D. J. Enright :
Poet of Humanism

D.J.ENRIGHT

Poet of Humanism

WILLIAM WALSH

Professor of Commonwealth Literature
University of Leeds

821
914
ENRIGHT

CAMBRIDGE UNIVERSITY PRESS

Published by the Syndics of the Cambridge University Press
Bentley House, 200 Euston Road, London NW1 2DB
American Branch: 32 East 57th Street, New York, N.Y. 10022

© Cambridge University Press 1974

Library of Congress Catalogue Card Number: 73 90814

ISBN 0 521 20383 X

First published 1974

Printed in Great Britain by
Western Printing Services Ltd, Bristol

FOR CLAUDE AND CHRISTINE BISSELL

CONTENTS

ACKNOWLEDGEMENT

I am grateful to the following for permission to quote material protected by copyright: D. J. Enright, Chatto and Windus, Heinemann, Secker and Warburg, Routledge and Kegan Paul. I am indebted to Chatto and Windus for permission to draw on my essay 'The Noodle-vendor's Flute' in *A Human Idiom* (1964).

November 1973   w. w.

I

CAREER

Dennis Joseph Enright was born on 11 March 1920, in Leamington, Warwickshire, to an Anglo-Irish family. His father was an ex-soldier 'obliged early in life to enlist in the British Army as a result of the premature death of his father, a Fenian'. He was also 'an absent-mindedly lapsed Catholic'. His English mother, though she also had a trace of Welsh in her, was 'vaguely a chapel-goer, but only because she felt the Church of England belonged to Them and was socially a cut above the likes of Us. (A primitive way of dividing up the world, perhaps, but events had generally borne it out.)'[1] Being brought up in a working-class family of mixed nationality, background, creed, has its disadvantages – not simply economic ones – but it had its advantages too. For one thing it deprived Enright pre-natally of 'the ability to comprehend religious or political ideologies, race, nationality and nationalism – phenomena', he observes drily, 'which one needs to have a firm grasp of if one is to lead a stable and balanced life'[2] in our present world. Enright's conception of a full and balanced life, as both his career and art confirm, was of a sort for which this 'deficiency' in training was the right preparation, the life of a poet requiring as it does a more gripping and less cloudy sense of reality. Not that there were not strains in his life as a child, consequences of poverty, of the early loss of a father, of having to be supported by an overworked mother, of a constricted milieu, and in his life in school, Leamington College, and a Midland community which he felt to be suffused with '. . .the. . . intense and petty concern for gentility. . .the habit of judging people by their most external manifestations. . .the sense of being stifled mentally and emotionally'.[3]

---

[1] *Memoirs of a Mendicant Professor*, London 1969, p. 103.
[2] Biographical material supplied for *Midcentury Authors*, a book forthcoming from H. W. Wilson and Co., New York.
[3] *Ibid.*

D. J. Enright: poet of humanism

Some forty years later, when as a well-known poet, writer, critic, Enright visited China, he watched in Canton a class of exquisitely behaved children, their eyes above protective gauze masks delicately averted from the unfortunate freak of a foreigner, receive a lesson of brutishly xenophobic propaganda, and he reflected on the brainwashing he had undergone at the age of these children.

Nothing half as carbolic as this, no – just that it was merely right and proper to die for your king and country, that when there wasn't a war there was unemployment which was less stirring and worse for the country, that on Empire Day you saluted the flag and sang a special hymn, that foreigners were silly and wicked, that too much reading was bad for the eyes and other parts of you as well, and that God intended you to abide in that state of life to which He had called you, with the exception of a few scholarship boys who would have to be eternally grateful to society for going against God on their behalf.[4]

Being a scholarship boy in the 1930s, as Enright himself was, carried with it a set of feelings which, with the expansion of higher education and the wider extension of the grant system, is hard now to grasp. It made one conscious of merit and independence – in the circumstances of the times, of a very considerable degree of both of these things certainly – but it also communicated a sense of the gratitude expected by the kindly institution and the magnanimous society in which it existed. Scholarships brought Enright to Cambridge where he read English at Downing as a pupil of F. R. Leavis, an experience which had a lasting influence upon his personal character and his critical practice – though I hasten to say, an *absorbed* influence. Enright has never been a dwarf Leavis or in any particular a stereotyped *Scrutineer*. Leavis impressed Enright as one of the very few teachers he had ever come across who actively and deeply wanted his pupils to follow what he was saying and who treated them as something approaching equals without a hint of condescension. '. . .I consider myself extremely lucky to have had as tutors both Leavis and James Smith, for Professor – as he now is – Smith had the gift of bringing out the most gauche of pupils by deceiving them into thinking that they were teaching him and that he was grateful for it.'[5]

Enright was an unusual undergraduate, remarkable not only for his academic promise but for a distinctive and early literary

[4] *Memoirs*, p. 200.
[5] *Conspirators and Poets*, London 1966, p. 31.

gift as well as for a singularly individual and attractive personality. Cambridge, the proper context for the development of these qualities, perhaps required at that time rather more than natural endowment. Certainly in these days such a person would have found himself very rapidly impelled up the academic escalator but at that time promise, particularly when it had realised itself at Downing and in *Scrutiny*, was by no means a guarantee of success, or even of work.

Life was hard then, in all sorts of ways. It was hard for 'scholarship boys' to get scholarships enough to enable them to go up to the university. It was hard to get published. It was difficult to start a magazine and difficult to keep it going. It was hard to find a post. Some experienced remarkable difficulty in obtaining promotion in their professions, or even security: in the 'Retrospect' appended to the reprint of *Scrutiny* Leavis mentions that it was not until he was 'well on into his fifties' that he at last achieved a full University Lectureship.[6] Today a lot of us are Professors, and most of us at any rate contrive to become full Lecturers well before our fifties. Professor Kermode, incidentally, remarks of *Scrutiny* that 'merely to appear in those pages, it seems, was to found a reputation'. Yes, but what sort of reputation? Paranoia does not loom large in my own make-up – I confess at once to a sense of having done rather better for myself in life than I deserve – so I can assure Professor Kermode, without any personal bitterness, that for a candidate for home university posts immediately after the war – let alone earlier – to have appeared in the pages of *Scrutiny* was considerably more disadvantageous than to have appeared in no pages at all. Some of us went abroad in the first case – and whether we afterwards regretted it is another matter – simply because foreign universities were less particular or (perhaps through backwardness) less prejudiced against *Scrutiny*'s minor fry. What it was like in the 'thirties and early 'forties I can only imagine – but I *can* imagine.

That the Establishment of today is so much more tolerant, or nervous, or splintered, or amorphous, may in part be the result of the hard and telling knocks which *Scrutiny* gave the Establishment of its time. Today nothing succeeds like satire, as the history of the Angry Young Men so aptly indicates. Voices crying in the wilderness are soon after to be heard echoing through the corridors of power. And the academic arena is more often given over to exhibitions of grunt-and-groan than to genuine battle. In the age of affluence and atomic anxiety the missionary spirit seems hard to come by and hard to hold. Today *Scrutiny* would receive a grant from some foundation or other, it would even be able to pay its contributors, probably. But whether anything really like *Scrutiny* would last for long these days is a more doubtful question.

The generation to which the present writer belongs has a foot in each of these two worlds, and there is small excuse for *us* if we forget the con-

---

[6] 'For the first half-dozen years of *Scrutiny* I had no post and no salary, and was hard put to it to make a living.' *Listener*, 1 November 1956.

ditions, the atmosphere, in which the Leavises lived and worked during their formative and perhaps their greatest years. You *had* to be devoted, you had to be tough, to survive in any serious and minority-supported endeavour in those days.[7]

Accordingly – after the above I feel that a more neutral word would muffle the correct tone – accordingly, Enright entered the profession, the university teaching of English Literature, to which he has devoted some thirty years, in Alexandria at the then Farouk I University. He worked in Egypt for four years. During that time he married Madeleine Harders, a French woman, a teacher of French Literature and a gifted painter. They have one daughter, Dominique, now an undergraduate at Oxford. He published in Alexandria a volume of verse, *Season Ticket*, from which only a small group was preserved for reprinting in his first English volume, *The Laughing Hyena*.[8] In his autobiographical note for *Midcentury Authors* Enright refers the reader to his novel *Academic Year*[9] for details of his life during this period, and certainly that novel, to which I shall return in due course, conveys in a remarkably mature and confident manner the experience of the English teacher in an Egyptian university of the time as well as his life outside. Bacon, Packet and Brett are three teachers of English at the University of Alexandria, who embody the experienced, the ardent and the intolerant in the English character, and present a kind of English solidity in the face of the aspiring and impalpable Egyptian sensibility. The novel is beautifully light in its touch and it contains scenes, on teaching and the conduct of examinations in the university, which are the pure milk of gaiety.[10] It may be that there is an inclination to reflect gently on the passage of events and that the action is seen through a slightly misted air. But the spirit of that melodramatic city with its horri-

[7] *Conspirators and Poets*, pp. 34–5.
[8] London 1953.
[9] London 1955.
[10] Cf. 'University Examinations in Egypt', in *The Laughing Hyena*.

The air is thick with nerves and smoke: pens tremble in sweating hands:
Domestic police flit in and out, with smelling salts and aspirin:
And servants, grave-faced but dirty, pace the aisles,
With coffee, Players and Coca-Cola.

Was it like this in my day, at my place? Memory boggles
Between the aggressive fly and curious ant – but did I really
Pause in my painful flight to light a cigarette or swallow drugs?

fying beggars, simple fellahin, its cotton-Pashas, the sophisticated society of its big houses, is evoked with success remarkable in a first book. As successful and rare is the wit. Indeed, the combination of liberality of spirit with an exquisite capacity for mocking anything grand or spiritually obese makes *Academic Year* a memorable experience for the reader. It is also, like the Egyptian poems in *The Laughing Hyena*, a fine distillation of that part of Enright's life.

The Voice

What is the mystery of the Orient? It is the Voice,
Its dimensions in space and time, its lack of inhibition.
After size of belly, size of progeny, and size of bank balance, size of voice
Is the worthy, awful thing: the monstrous mark of Godhead.

No, it is not the tram that is quiet, it is the passengers
Who possess the Voice. No, it is not the Revolution at last,
It is two who possess the Voice, saying good day to each other.
No, it is not a village Cassandra predicting a slump in cotton,
It is a female of the Voice, keening some distant relative whom she never
    met.

And as the thermometer rises, so does the Voice. In August,
When the body lies slumped in the shade, you still will meet
The Voice, boldly parading the burning streets. Oh,
More monumental than old Egypt's pyramids is its Voice!

And yet to what small end! Listen, my Egyptian friends,
I have heard a voice more powerful than yours, one that carries further
And shakes down houses. I heard it in a smart café,
Whispering some short sly European phrase.

It was in Alexandria in 1948 that Enright first evinced, publicly at any rate, that capacity or instinct for tripping lightly into disaster,[11] whether comic or cruel, which has been a feature of his career in half a dozen countries. The occasion could hardly have been more proper, a Sunday afternoon stroll with an Irish colleague along the Corniche to take tea with the Professor of Modern History and his wife. A bored bystander, a crowd less than well-disposed to extraneous elements, shouts of 'Jewish spies' and they were arrested by a small scared policeman. The police station was 'a little squalid hell of its own, smelling of urine, with

---

[11] 'The Fairies', in *Addictions*, London 1962.
>   Hard up at the time, the fairies gave me
>   what they could: the gift
>   Of laying the right hand on the wrong door-knob.

women squatting in the corridors weeping noisily for their arrested husbands or sons, and policemen pruriently unwinding their bandages to compare the wounds they had acquired in the course of the last student demonstrations. Here and there were gargantuan play-pens, crammed with prisoners vociferously declaring their own innocence and the guilt of others.' There was the usual bawling interrogation by a lieutenant who had studied his role in a B-feature film. 'When did you swim ashore from that Jewish ship?' Rescue was effected by a clerk in the University administration who was one of a large group of admirers having coffee with the lieutenant's superior, all of them exclaiming 'over the latter's wisdom, his power, his wealth and probably his sexual potency too'. Drama collapsed into farce when Enright and his friend, stumbling out of the police station, suggested that as the police had made them late for their appointment, they might like to stand them a taxi: an idea that brought the house down. Later, a tip that he was being watched by the Secret Police explained 'why I had kept coming across those outstanding personages, uncommonly noble of visage and bearing, large and healthy-looking, carrying pastoral staffs, whom I had vaguely taken for the Moslem equivalent of dandyish Roman cardinals or for Egyptian landowners who disdained to wear foreign dress'.[12] A month later he was summoned to the University administration where it was apologetically explained that he had fallen under suspicion because on the question relating to religion on the entry form he had declared himself a Wesleyan Methodist. It was explained that *They* thought it might be something Jewish. Feeling like an apostate, Enright changed it to Church of England and the Secret Police lost all interest in him.

There were to be similar episodes dotted over Enright's career, some as daft as the Egyptian one, like the encounter with the man-eating landlady in Berlin, others as maddening, like those collisions with prudent British diplomats and flinching cultural officers, some more sinister, like the interview with the Acting Minister for Labour and Law in Singapore in 1960, who threatened him with immediate deportation because of a set of pretty orthodox remarks on the nature of culture in – of all things – an Inaugural Lecture on 'Robert Graves and the Decline of Modernism', or the wholly irrational and terrifying beating-up by a dozen policemen in Bangkok when Enright was on his way

[12] *Memoirs*, p. 104.

home with his wife from a friend's birthday party. Each of them shows how an innocent and homely context can be transformed by suspicion into a cage of violence, whether physical or moral; each of them shows Enright's gift for being a bit of grit in the administrative eye; each of them shows his inability to be washed out of that organ without protest; each of them shows him as a victim but not a suave or accommodating one: a sardonic wit keeps him from slipping into a merely dignified silence.

In 1950 Enright left Alexandria, city of 'agile, giggling Arabs', where even the lock-up had a human atmosphere, 'with its grand noisy emotions, its Old-Testament way of doing nothing by halves', for Birmingham, where

> the clouds,
> Slow and resolved and brutal, shroud
> All the damp statues in all the cramped squares.[13]

He moved from lecturing to Egyptian undergraduates, which, while it must have had its disconcerting passages, was always lively and engaging, to the bleak and testing work of teaching adults in the evening in many places in classes organised by the Extramural Department of Birmingham University. Like all work of this kind it was hard, underpaid and valuable, taking place at the point at which academics touch the world outside the university directly and effectively. It was during this time that he was composing the poems which appeared in *The Laughing Hyena*, and learning to speak in that personal voice and with that idiosyncratic vision which give the impression of possessing very vividly the quality of currency, the air of registering this world at this moment, and of rising out of and being addressed to our perplexities as they now are. Already in these early poems Enright shows a bias towards light and intelligibility,[14] unusual at the time, a gift for

---

[13] 'Autumn Sunday in Birmingham', in *The Laughing Hyena*.
[14] Which is why I try to write lucidly, that even I
  Can understand it – and mildly, being loth to face the fashionable
                                                        terrors,
  Or venture among sinister symbols, under ruin's shadow.
  Once having known, at an utter loss, that utter incomprehension
  – Unseen, unsmelt, the bold bat, the cloud of jasmine,
  Truly out of one's senses – it is unthinkable
  To drink horror from ink, to sink into the darkness of words –
  Words one has chosen oneself. Poems, at least,
  Ought not to be phantoms.
            ('Life and Letters', in *The Laughing Hyena*.)

divining in the current, shabby language natural vivacities, suppleness of tone, and a habit of treating a serious subject in a comedian's manner. Even so early in his career as this we see one who celebrates in an individual and wholly contemporary voice the human virtues of hope and charity.

It was a personality, of which these qualities are the natural expression, that Enright brought to bear upon his experience of Japan, where he was to spend the years from 1953 to 1956 teaching at the private Kōnan University near Kobe. His vision of Japan articulated sharply in *The World of Dew: Aspects of Living Japan*,[15] and more profoundly in poems in *Bread rather than Blossoms*[16] and *Some Men are Brothers*,[17] is as different from Lafcadio Hearn's, a frozen, aesthetic vase, as it is from the economist's current view of the industrial giant. It takes its stand on the very strong and simple, but also difficult and evasive, proposition that Japan like any other state is to be judged on human grounds and in the belief that civilisation has to do with the diminution of the traces of human tears. In both Japanese history and sensibility Enright found something almost like a grudge against the merely human. The unusually complicated system of Japanese behaviour appears to be based not on a recognition but on a proud and yet pathetic denial of humanity. The Japanese set themselves intolerably high standards and the severest restrictions and broke away from them in fits of sudden and desperate violence. 'Unable to forgive others they have resorted to assassination; unable to forgive themselves they have turned to suicide, in its most agonising forms.'[18] Their art, similarly, has the most fragmentary and tenuous connection with human life, its beauties are those of strict stylisation, the faces in its painting washed clean of all feeling, the gap between its poetry and its ordinary life wider than that of any other race. The Japanese object was to become either a god or, if that proved impossible, a work of art. All Enright's sympathies, in a society which showed this formalised animus against common humanity, were on the side of the young Japanese, 'whether the young writer, the young man in the street or the young woman who manages to keep off the streets'. [19] It was his sympathy and his strenuously human concern which made Enright in Japan as elsewhere so rare a teacher of

[15] London 1955.   [16] London 1956.
[17] London 1960.   [18] *The World of Dew*, p. 15.
[19] *Ibid.* p. 21.

students. Modest in aim – 'I have no wish. . .to take into my hands the springs of their being. They are neither tap-water nor plasticine'[20] – erudite and witty, a bit of a clown, feeling himself always in the presence of another human being, he was able, as I myself have observed in visiting universities in Singapore, in India and even in Britain, where he has taught, to affect the young deeply and significantly.

On Enright's first day in Japan one of his future pupils came to see him looking intensely worried, an expression which he later became accustomed to. ' "We do not know what to call you," he blurted out. "Call me what you like, within limits." "Might we. . .could we," he asked timidly, "call you 'sir'?" "By all means – why not?" (After all, "sir" is a more neutral title than *sensei*;[21] and somehow or other the latter is rarely bestowed upon foreign teachers, I suspect.) "Well, sir," he explained in a relieved tone, "the Americans told us that we should not call anybody sir." '[22] It was students like these, including those with rented tape recorders, paid for by the sale of blood to Transfusion Centres, who came to snatch a free lesson from the horse's mouth or to get Enright to record in his pure and undefiled English the second half of *Black Beauty* or the first half of the *Private Papers of Henry Ryecroft* and who took disinclination as a curious foreign joke to be smiled at and disregarded: it was students like these and bar girls like Akichan, with a child, an old mother and a bed-ridden consumptive husband to support, who with others of her kind seemed to him instances of the most arrant, most heart-breaking wastage of human goodness, who made up for the other aspects of living Japan like 'the blank unbridgeable chasm between an exquisite sensitivity towards the arts and a stolid insensitivity towards human suffering',[23] or again what was expressed in the

[20] *Memoirs*, p. 179.
[21] *Sensei.* 'A magic word, and yet very equivocal. *Sensei* means "teacher" plus "scholar" plus "beloved master"; it means intellect, learning, culture, taste; it means China, *tanka*, *haiku*, Nō plays, pottery, Zen. It means head in the clouds, hermit, thinker. Yet it also means "those who can't do, teach", a reciter of old lecture notes, the over-worked and under-paid servant of a government institution or a private corporation, a man who hasn't the wit to grow rich by shifting theoretical money from one bank to another, the uneasy tenant of an Ivory Tower that an atom bomb has fallen on.' (*The World of Dew*, p. 24.)
[22] *Ibid.* p. 58.
[23] *Memoirs*, p. 38.

9

awful fight to get on or off trains, 'the collision at the door between those desiring to leave and those desiring to enter, the mild noises of distress from those being trampled underfoot and the mild noises of impersonal deprecation from those doing the trampling'.[24] Students and bar girls, universities and bars, bulk large in Enright's recorded memories of Japan, as he himself observes. The reason, he explains, is that the middle-class in Japan, like the middle-class elsewhere, remained secret and detached. But another figure which he met on a cold night in 1955, swathed from head to ankles in straw, remained in his mind. He has tried, he says, 'to exorcise [it] by means of poems written at intervals ever since, but without success.'

> What did I fear the most?
> To ignore and bustle past?
> To acknowledge and perhaps
> Find out what best was lost?[25]

In 1956 Enright went as *Gastdozent* to the Free University of West Berlin, under the auspices of the British Council. When he had gone from Egypt to Japan he noticed an interesting difference in the characteristic misuses of English of Japanese and Egyptian students. 'My experience has been that those of the Egyptians are predominantly comic in spirit – slovenly, a bit brutish, cavalier, unpredictable but yielding to elucidation, orotund and occasionally superb. Those of the Japanese, on the other hand, are predominantly tragic – contorted, agonized, tight-lipped, sometimes baffling, consistent and insistent, and occasionally poetic in a gently sad sort of way.'[26] When he went from Japan to Germany he noticed a different kind of difference. The bad public behaviour of the Japanese had often disturbed and angered him. The good public behaviour of the Germans he found more acutely alarming. 'Disorder along with charm is feasible; order accompanied by politeness is highly acceptable. But order along with a stupid un-couthness is intolerable.'[27] In Germany, to start with, he was regarded by his colleagues at the Free University as an academic nobody, foisted upon them, perhaps for sinister reasons, by the British Military Government. In the eyes of the British Military Government, on the other hand, he was regarded as a slightly seedy non-member of that organisation, car-less, sports-jacketed

[24] *Ibid.* p. 39.
[25] *Ibid.* p. 37.
[26] *The World of Dew*, p. 97.
[27] *Memoirs*, p. 58.

10

and long haired, and moreover as an apolitical person of liberal
views he was thought to shade dangerously close to the Communist
line. Certainly the views of his German colleagues changed. They
wanted him to stay on an extended appointment, and some 21
months later, when he had left Bangkok in peculiar circumstances,
he was offered an extraordinary professorship at the Free University. But both Berlin and the University affected him unhappily.
Although he was living in what was said to be a most exciting
place at a most significant time, it turned out to be spiritually
deadening and as exciting as the Leamington Spa of his childhood.
The relations between staff and students in the Free University
were distant and slight, those between the lower and higher grades
of staff hardly more intimate. Freedom was more an element in
the title of the institution than a quality of the life. He tried in a
number of poems to capture the atmosphere of Berlin, but the
note that appears is either of horrified oppression at the stony
strangulation of the city, or a sardonic awareness of an other than
human combination of cleanliness and efficiency.

> In no country
> Are the disposal services more efficient.
>
> Standardised dustbins
> Fit precisely into the mouth of a large cylinder
> Slung on a six-wheeled chassis.
> Even the dustbin lid is raised mechanically
> At the very last moment.
> You could dispose of a corpse like this
> Without giving the least offence.
>
> In no country
> Are the public lavatories more immaculately kept.
> As neat as new pins, smelling of pine forests,
> With a roar like distant Wagner
> Your sins are washed away.[28]

Japan could provoke resentment, Berlin antagonism; but Siam,
the next station in Enright's mendicant professoriate, where he
became Professor of English at Chulalongkorn University, Bangkok, could produce no reaction of that kind: 'a light, fragrant,
mollifying oil flowed over everything'.[29] Not that Enright sub-
scribed to the view which holds the Thais to be a simple, innocent,

[28] 'No Offence', in *Some Men are Brothers*.
[29] *Memoirs*, p. 72.

cheerful race. Japanese behaviour makes them seem more extraordinary and perplexing than they are, that of the Thais makes them seem more ordinary and comprehensible than in fact they are. In pursuit of understanding by mistake, or misdirection, Enright, characteristically, offers in his memoirs an exercise in his technique or fieldwork based on the analysis of students' howlers and pseudo-howlers. Here are a few examples of the very pretty clutch he adduces:

If the poet always sings the truth, he would have a little raw material to produce his work because there are not much truths.

'Fear no more the heat o' the sun' means: now we have air-conditioning.

Shakespeare was the great oppressive figure in Elizabethan period.

A ballad usually consists of four lines and jealousy.

I like to read poems as much as sleeping.

Milton was Puritan so he did not believe in God very much.

Shakespeare was genius in creating the quiverful quotation.

Reading poetry makes you nice and neat.

Thai literature is full of detailed description of sexual act, which English literature is not. Or perhaps I have not read enough.

Enright finds a handsome consistency in Thai mistakes. Thais are realistic, taking a modest Buddhist view of 'this world of dew, this world of small expectations'.[30] There are but few truths available in this life and the Thais are in happy but not arrogant possession of most of them. Literature is charming but we ought to take only a sober view of its importance, in comparison with genuinely significant things, Buddhism, the monarchy, food, rest, and being neat and nice. Neatness and niceness are functions of that quality – grace Enright calls it rather than spirituality – in which Eastern peoples, and certainly the Thais, show themselves as truly our superiors. 'Grace of bearing, often of feature (their faces do not wear out as soon as ours), grace in everyday affairs, in their superficial relationships (so long as nothing untoward intervenes) and in their most intimate relationships.'[31]

There was to be a violent distortion in Enright's doctrine of

[30] *Ibid.* p. 75.   [31] *Ibid.* p. 83.

Thai grace before he left the country. But till then not much interrupted what, from another point of view, might be called a period of grace. One experience possible then, not now, which Enright engaged in regularly was the smoking of opium. In his view moderate opium smoking by a healthy person of good-quality opium is not only harmless but pleasant and even beneficial. Such smoking has nothing to do with the current practice of drug taking, 'the pumping of filthy chemicals into the veins', which is a variety of masturbation, whereas opium smoking in the Thai way has 'its effects, happens within, one's relations with other people and the outside world'. It is characteristic of Enright's temperament that he sees a practice many other writers have taken to be exotic, mysterious and even mystical, as a mild, even a commonplace affair. It was an experience productive for him of no images of damsels, domes and dulcimers, no unimaginable Coleridgean ecstasies, but simply of images of what was there, 'a grubby, badly lighted, stuffy shack'. The atmosphere of the shack, or den, compared to the rest of Bangkok night life as a Victorian parlour to a stroll in Soho. It was filled with a kind of English Sabbath somnolence and it suggested to Enright nothing so much as a rather quiet and thoughtful working men's club. The place was bleak and physically comfortless, but it was one in which – rare in Bangkok – everyone was equal and where no one represented anything but himself, a singular condition in a city where expatriates were invariably representatives of something or other, of SEATO, or ECAFE, or FAO, or JUSMAG, or USOM. 'To put it simply, one felt pretty well at home there. It was a good place to go once a week or so for cleaning and repair work.' (Perhaps I should report that since leaving Thailand Enright has taken nothing stronger or more unorthodox than a couple of aspirins or a half a Soneryl tablet when hard-pressed for sleep.)

On 1 July 1959, the military government of Marshal Sarit decreed the closing of the licensed opium dens and the burning of the pipes. Here are lines from a poem Enright wrote to record that event:

> Who had imagined they were government property? –
> Wooden cylinders with collars of silver, coming
> From China, brown and shiny with sweat and age.
> Inside them were banks of dreams, shiny with
> Newness, though doubtless of time-honoured stock.
> They were easy to draw on: you pursed your lips

As if to suckle and sucked your breath as if to
Sigh: two skills which most of us have mastered.

The dreams themselves weren't government property.
Rather, the religion of the people. While the state
Took its tithes and the compliance of sleepers.
Now a strong government dispenses with compliance,
A government with rich friends has no need of tithes.

What acrid jinn was it that entered their flesh?
For some, a magic saucer, over green enamelled
Parks and lofty flat-faced city offices, to
Some new Tamerlane in his ticker-tape triumph –
Romantics! They had been reading books.
Others found the one dream left them: dreamless sleep.

As for us, perhaps we had eaten too much to dream,
To need to dream, I mean, or have to sleep.
For us, a moment of thinking our thoughts were viable,
And hope not a hopeless pipe-dream; for us
The gift of forgiveness for the hole in the road,
The dog we ran over on our way to bed.
Wasn't that something? The Chinese invented so much. . .[32]

The useful, fragrant life in Bangkok concluded senselessly in a
bout of violence, a calm domestic occasion erupting into craziness.
Returning home from a friend's birthday party with his wife,
Enright found the road blocked just before his house by an empty
car which had one of its doors open. He drew up, his wife closed
the door, and they drove past. At this moment more than a dozen
drunken policemen rushed from a neighbouring house (which had
been a brothel of long and good standing, unknown to the
Enrights and to the wife of the British official who found the house
for them) and under the impression that the Enrights had done
damage to their car, brutally set about them. Enright, badly
beaten up, was thrust into the cage at the local police station,
which indeed he found a peaceful and friendly place, not unlike the
opium den. One old lag offered him a bald tyre to sit on, another
a stick of mosquito-repelling incense. A bad-tempered Consular
official arrived during the night and had him transferred to an
office, where he was guarded by policemen with rifles. The police
officer, now undrunk, was alarmed when it was discovered that
Enright was indeed a professor and not a local thug or 'cowboy'
as they were called. But the officer's readiness to retract his com-

[32] 'The Burning of the Pipes', in *Addictions*.

plaint was dissipated when he found the British Consul only too
ready to placate him with the assurance of an apology. It was
noted that this apology was given 'with an ill grace'. That ill
grace and disgrace should end both the doctrine of grace and the
period of grace is sad but not unusual, particularly in Enright's
life. The Thais themselves were horrified by what happened to
Enright. They had no desire to lose so good and liked and free a
teacher. They were also baffled since they couldn't see that being
roughed-up by their police was a stain on anybody's character.
But Enright was employed by the British Council and so they
could not prevent his withdrawal. On the other hand Chulalongkorn University immediately itself invited him back as a member
of its own staff to be paid for by the university. But Thailand was
now spoilt.

This whole episode taught me a useful lesson, something which I had
been in danger of forgetting as I called at the Embassy commissary to
collect my tax-free liquor and smokes – if you live abroad, then live
abroad, and don't slip into the bad habit of remembering you are an
Englishman on those occasions when you think it will work to your
advantage. I had sent my nasty little poems to England by the diplomatic
bag – and now justice both diplomatic and poetic had been rendered me.
Writers, above all, ought to know that where they are concerned there is no
such thing as diplomatic privilege.[33]

The ambiguous complexities of British official behaviour are
interestingly illustrated in this case, both in Bangkok and in
London. Accommodating himself sinuously to the prevailing
pressures, one Consular official apologises on behalf of an innocent
person for the crime of being beaten up by the police – or perhaps
just for his tactlessly having been there; the British Embassy, on
Enright's appeal, disowns him; a cultural official explains that
having dragged the name of the British Council in the mud and
ruined his own career he must leave the country on the next plane;
in London a group of benign senior officials kindly explain that
he had been the victim of officially improper behaviour, that he
would continue to receive his salary and do various little jobs
for the Council; no such jobs turn up and Enright gets used to the
sad, patient look on the faces of various deskbound home officers
'when they saw the Ancient Mariner, the scarred old soldier
prematurely retired from the field, peering ominously through
their door'; the Director-General summons Enright to say he

[33] *Memoirs*, pp. 107–8.

gathers that Enright had written a book (a novel called *Insufficient Poppy*, in the press at the time and published in 1960) which was not the sort of book the British Council could have their officers writing, and while it had been fortunate to have his services in the past it would not be able to avail itself of them in the future; on another floor of the same building he is invited to take part in a lecture tour of Indian universities:

It was a strange place, that building in Davies Street, and perhaps it still is. A blessing on its head! Cringing one's way out of one office, a broken man, an exposed pornographer, whoremonger, dipsomaniac and opium addict, one's painter torn to ribbons, one would enter another office to find oneself a hero of labour, an expert, a distinguished academic, besought on almost bended knees to be gracious enough to fly first class to India and spread one's sweetness and light. . .[34]

On the other hand, as Enright realised, this gap in monolithic unity was perhaps one of the good things about British habits and procedures. It saves the private person from total administrative blacking. It does enable him to receive some of the rewards of accidental virtues as well as the wages of uncommitted crimes.

If this was a blow from the Right Enright was soon to be sent reeling by the Left in a way that shows the wretched proneness of the liberal humanist to accident and scandal: of the genuine and sensitive one, that is, many who profess the appellation being notoriously unprone, at least as we see in Britain, in fact, to anything but an apparently well-padded success. In 1960 Enright was appointed Johore Professor of English in the University of Malaya at Singapore, as it was then known, while he was in Delhi on the first leg of the Indian tour, a post he had been offered two years earlier but had been unable to accept because of his undertaking to go to Bangkok. In November of that year he delivered his Inaugural Lecture on the fairly severe academic topic 'Robert Graves and the Decline of Modernism'. As is the custom on these occasions he prefaced the more technical part of his lecture with some general comments, and naturally enough, since the context was Singapore, he allowed himself some animadversions on the state of culture in the country. The government at the time, in accordance with its somewhat governessy and authoritative manner, was engaged in an effort to wipe out what it called Yellow Culture, a large and ill-defined concept which ranged from 'juke boxes to Wordsworth's daffodils. . .and for a time,

[34] *Ibid*, p. 113.

16

myself. . .'[35] Enright advanced the proposition with characteristic point and lucidity that culture was something that could not be legislated into being but had to be constructed by 'people listening to music and composing it, reading books and writing them, looking at pictures and painting them, and observing life and living it'.[36] Culture, which began not in a test tube but in the foul rag and bone shop of the heart, had to be produced by people left free to make their own mistakes, to suffer and to discover. This light, liberal voice was interpreted, with the help of the local newspaper, as an offensive intervention into the affairs of the State. Enright was summoned before the Acting Minister for Labour and Law and berated loudly in Malay, which was then translated for his benefit by another Minister. The private rebuke was accompanied by a public scolding which informed him that should he again wander from the bounds of the work for which he was allowed entry into the country, his professional visit pass would be cancelled. He was being paid handsomely to do the job, the Minister asserted, which he was presumably qualified to do, and not to enter into the field of local politics which he was unqualified in. 'The days are gone when birds of passage from Europe or elsewhere used to make it a habit of participating from their superman heights of European civilization.'[37] Throughout the interview there was to Enright's Bangkok-sensitised nostrils a faint whiff of rubber truncheons in the background. The students in the university protested on Enright's behalf and the staff entered into a series of meetings, in the academic way, which diffused themselves in scholarly talk. 'If you are in trouble', is Enright's mordant advice, 'throw yourself on the mercy of the nearest peasant, publican or policeman, but never go to an academic: you will be dead long before he has finished formulating his attitude towards you and your problem.'[38] Enright stubbornly stayed on, in spite of much well-meant advice to leave on his high horse, and a formula of reconciliation was elaborated in the following letters:[39]

From Enright:

Dear Minister,
   I shall be glad to elucidate some of the comments in the preliminary passages of my inaugural lecture on 'Robert Graves and the Decline of

[35] *Ibid.* p. 122.   [36] *Ibid.* p. 125.   [37] *Ibid.* p. 129.
[38] *Ibid.* pp. 137–8.   [39] *Ibid.* pp. 139–40.

Modernism', delivered in the University on 17 November and tendentiously reported in the Press.

In these introductory remarks I spoke of culture in general, meaning by that word 'the production and consumption of art'. In a local reference, I gave my view that, as a lively modern state and an open port, Singapore should remain culturally open, and thus gradually build up its own modern and appropriate culture. No sneers at Malay art or the Malay way of life as such were intended.

I can assure you that I have not the slightest desire to comment on or interfere in the political issues of this country, of which – as you have pointed out – I am not a citizen.

> I remain, Minister,
> etc.

From the Minister:

Dear Sir,

I refer to your letter of 23rd November in reply to my letter of 18th November.

If you had so stated your position at our first meeting in the afternoon of the 18th November, my letter to you would not have been necessary. But I am glad you agree that your status as a teacher in the University does not clothe you with the rights of a citizen to comment on or participate in the political issues of the country.

However, let me assure you that your right to teach your subject and to expound your views within your province of learning is completely unfettered.

Since my letter to you of 18th November has been made public, it would be necessary that your reply and this letter should also be published.

> Yours faithfully,
> etc.

The affair continued to rumble on in the press and in the university and in the country. Indeed, Enright was moved years later to protest about being taken, particularly by the staff of the university, as a symbol of academic freedom in its quarrels with an increasingly intrusive government:

Academic freedom and university autonomy are worth fighting for, I believe, because if they are not fought for then they will go by the board entirely – to the detriment, in the long run, of the University, the students and staff, and the country. But they should be fought for on firm and on firmly remembered ground. They are real, and not – what 'the Enright affair' has become – mythical.[40]

To be taken for a symbol was distasteful to one who had learnt to become suspicious about the symbolic function. In Japan

[40] Letter to the *Straits Times*, July 1966.

Enright had seen how successful the thistledown of symbolism could be in disguising not only wretchedness but reality:

> The garden is not a garden, it is an
>   expression of Zen;
> The trees are not rooted in earth, then:
>   they are rooted in Zen.
> And this Tea has nothing to do with thirst:
> It says the unsayable. And this bowl
>   is no vessel: it is the First
> And the Last, it is the Whole.
>
> Beyond the bamboo fence are life-size people,
> Rooted in precious little, without benefit of
>   philosophy,
> Who grow the rice, who deliver the goods, who
> Sometimes bear the unbearable. They too
>   drink tea, without much ceremony. . .[41]

Enright's bias in favour of the actual had been strengthened by his experience of the literary world:

> One thinks of those critics for whom the outside
>   is a dreadful bore:
> they scrape for the ambiguous, dig for the profound,
>   deep, deep beneath the ground –
> what you read on the surface of the agitated page
>   is only an idle dusty weed.[42]

One also thinks of what Enright describes as 'the consistent and blank lack of interest in my subject-matter, the utter incuriosity on this score – for me, the important one'.[43] One of the reasons, therefore, why Enright came to have so deep an affection for the Chinese of Singapore, and particularly for the students through whom he increasingly sensed the character of the place, was that this 'collection of urbane and spiritually affluent individuals' was properly sceptical both of symbols and grand abstractions like freedom and independence. The Chinese are an honest, pragmatic race, hewing a middle line, lucid of mind, unworried by the mysteriousness of life. Without romantic expectations, 'they combine the stoical inwardness of the East with the sociably relaxed exterior of the West. Westernly progressive, they approve of family planning; Easternly philoprogenitive, they approve of

---

[41] 'Tea Ceremony', in *Bread rather than Blossoms.*
[42] 'The Interpreters', *ibid.*
[43] *Memoirs*, p. 189.

babies. In a Western way they believe in ideas and creeds, symposia and forums; in an Eastern way –

> To die for one's own belief
> What is it, but murder
> By one's child?

– they believe in survival.'[44]

Enright's career offers plenty of evidence for supposing that he must have on occasion doubted his own capacity for survival. If he did so, the Chinese he admired so much provided him with a model of indestructibility he succeeded in living up to. He survived for some ten years at Singapore before leaving finally in 1970 for London, to work in literary journalism and publishing – survived, as he puts it in a characteristic modulation of Joyce's formula, 'by dint of silence, exile, cunning, hysterics, sloth, low posture (as the sociologists call it) and simple-mindedness', and in spite of official disapproval which still operated at the lower, administrative level long after it was forgotten at the summit. Of course, he did more than survive in his graceful, mordant, almost oriental way. He soldiered on, serving his university with distinction and bringing to bear upon his students an intelligently humane, disinterested and disconcertingly non-mandarin influence. Above all he matured as a poet, developing a uniquely personal purity of style, extending his scope and preserving in a world working constantly against it an incorruptible wholeness and truth of self.

[44] *Ibid.* p. 181.

POETRY I
1953-60

Becoming a poet in the 1950s must have been one of the severest disciplines anyone could put himself to. That difficult, dangerous period when a talent is forming had to be passed in a time governed more than most by fictions of status, affluence, acceptance. A sensibility had to be constructed not in a society whose system ran with and supported a current of genuine life but in a marshmallow world with convictions hardly robust enough either to accept or reject. But if it was hard, it wasn't unpopular. There was a clutch of poets who began to arrive in the 1950s. They called themselves *The Movement*. But I am inclined to think that what they had in common wasn't motion – they had no agreed point of departure and certainly no concerted destination – but rather a posture, a negative stance.

> After so many (in so many places) words,
> It came to this one, No.
> Epochs of parakeets, of peacocks, of paradisiac birds –
> Then one bald owl croaked, No.
>
> ('Saying no')[1]

These young poets who depended above all on a freshness of contact with actuality, but who lived in a world infatuated with illusion, developed, had to develop, a cool evasive skill and an aptness in the tactics of disengagement. This was part of the success many of them had in devising a sensibility in keeping with the times, together with the voice through which it could be projected. The sensibility was agile and fluent, the voice casual and intelligently modulated. There was nothing stark or grand in the one, nothing inflatedly poetic in the other. A detached and modest manner, a dry decency of feeling, an utterance, in which, at its best, the contours of the verse are fitted exactly to the curves of contemporary speech – these are the marks of a

---

[1] *Some Men are Brothers.*

poetry which strikes the reader as being authentically and altogether naturally modern.

There are, of course, traces in these poets of strain and youth and earlier manners – the jagged and impeded line, the blatantly cerebral energy, the laborious construction. But in all of them at their best, and especially in the one who seems to me one of the most individual in character and most representative of the times, the poetical movement is light and gliding and unreluctant. Here are some lines from 'The Laughing Hyena by Hokusai'[2] which show the skilful manoeuvring of a liquid, lively rhythm:

For him it seems everything was molten. Court-ladies flow in gentle streams,
Or, gathering lotus, strain sideways from the curving boat,
A donkey prances, or a kite dances in the sky, or soars like sacrificial smoke.
All is flux; waters fall and leap, and bridges leap and fall.
Even his Tortoise undulates, and his Spring Hat is lively as a pool of fish.

The events of the poet's life play an important part in a poetry which has a solidly objective character. On the whole the poets of the 1950s do not look on a sequence of poems as a variety of poses best calculated to display aspects of the fascinating ego. Enright himself, as I have explained, has spent most of his career since Cambridge abroad, and this international experience seems to have a peculiar relevance to modern life. To be so closely in touch with the intelligent young of several countries gives access to a sensitive part of the modern world: as a teacher of a self-conscious generation he is in direct touch with people's intimately human concerns; as a post-imperial Englishman his human shape is unmuffled by the toga, his relationships undistorted by the hypocrisies of power or obedience. He writes in 'Entrance Visa':[3]

We were the Descendancy. Hurt but not surprised.
Atoning for our predecessors' every oath and sneer,
We paid in poverty the rich men's debt.

With no pretensions but to be human (both a modest and a gigantic ambition), the poet is qualified to join a dozen communities in as many lands. To say that he joins is perhaps too strong a way to describe his relation to the community. He is aware of the sense in which each place is for him only 'a change of homelessness'; and he has to preserve that measure of detach-

[2] *The Laughing Hyena.*   [3] *Some Men are Brothers.*

ment necessary for the attentive and adequate observer. On the other hand, wearing no more than the nakedness, the anonymity, of humanity and being also 'a perpetual refugee' may well be the essential entrance visas into many countries, as well as the most difficult to secure. So much of the poetry of the 1950s is like this, the poetry of the observant wanderer who, wherever he is, always cunningly sites himself to catch some eloquent notation of the human scene. A mere list of subjects from one of Enright's books, *Some Men are Brothers*, will suggest something of the variety of the world seen by this sharp contemporary eye and something of the agility with which the observer-poet gets into position: sitting in a German park, meeting an Egyptian at a cocktail party, Berlin dustbins and funeral facilities, a noodle-vendor's flute, Mr Yamashiro-no-Shōjō who is declared a Human National Treasure, a barge full of rice, a kite flight, a Japanese story (1687) called *The Conspectus of Sodomites*, the last male quagga left alive.

The poet's glance, we can tell from his treatment of these subjects, wry and original as it is, is bent upon reality. The existence of these 'sad and naughty persons', their odd and slippery jobs, their ambiguous yet appealing relationships, is fully and firmly established – and with the minimum of descriptive reference. (These poems are quite unpadded, and rest elegantly on nothing more than their own bones.) Disciplined observation, we realise, can be a remarkably productive poetic instrument; it is, indeed, an important and neglected human power.

> The flame-tree shames us, one and all:
> for what fit audience, though few, do we afford?
>
> ('A Day in an Undisciplined Garden')[4]

And to notice a thing with the poet's fine, unblurred particularity is to rescue it from falling into the refuse of life.

> If we do not observe, who will?
> Will anything observe or mourn for us?
>
> ('Insects')[5]

The observation of the poet is not, of course, the neutrality of the mirror. It depends upon a particular attitude and carries a special tone. In Enright's case as with most of these poets the attitude is pitying, the tone ironic.

[4] *Ibid.*   [5] *Ibid.*

D. J. Enright: poet of humanism

Only one subject to write about: pity.
Self-pity: the only subject to avoid.
How difficult to observe both conditions!
('How right they were, the Chinese poets')[6]

The pity is without the least taint of *de haut en bas*; it is a level, unfussy feeling, of which the impulse is seeing in another's plight an extension of one's own and recognising his nature within one's own self. It is an acknowledgement of the common thing in men: 'And being common/Therefore something rare indeed.' 'Men are brothers', murmurs this voice, lucidly, lovingly, a simplicity which is immediately corrected to a more astringent, complicated comment, 'Some men are brothers.' The peculiar flavour of these poems comes from combining the mild (a favourite word of this poet), the mild taste of charity with the acrid one of 'real cities, real houses, real time'.

Enright's poetry, I am convinced, is deeply serious. I am aware in it, for all its spry and modern matter, of a traditional – not a conventional – wholesomeness of feeling, and for all its mobility of manner, of a steadiness of moral centre. But I hope I have not suggested that it is in any way solemn. It also shows, like much modern writing, the disillusioned urchin grimacing behind a respectable back or the dead-pan peasant pulling the Unesco Fellow's leg. This poet, it is clear from his poetry – quite apart from his other writings – is a man of considerable learning, even *gravitas*; he is also, equally clearly, an outrageously mischievous comic: Johnson and Boswell curiously sharing a single skin. This is a blend of temperaments which is very much of the present and decidedly attractive. Perhaps the best figure for this sensibility is the subject of one of his own poems, 'The Noodle-Vendor's Flute',[7] an ingenious device, 'merely a rubber-bulb and metal horn', made like this to keep the lips from being frozen by the night winds. In itself it is a kind of snook cocked at a more literary flute. It cries the vendor's wares as he cycles from spot to spot on the look-out for manholes and late drunks, and it is the accompaniment, like most poetry in the 1950s, to the difficult and rather comic business of making a living.

> The puffing vendor, surer than a trumpet,
> Tells us we are not alone.
> Each night that same frail midnight tune

---

[6] *Bread rather than Blossoms.*   [7] *Some Men are Brothers.*

24

Squeezed from a bogus flute,
Under the noise of war, after war's noise,
It mourns the fallen, every night,
It celebrates survival –
In real cities, real houses, real time.

An accompaniment to the difficult and rather comic business
of making a living – yes. But also an accompaniment to the difficult, comic business of living itself. For it is living which interests
this poet, not life; not the portentous abstraction but its multiple
definitions. 'To live is compulsory'; one isn't free to take up an
attitude or to have large assumptions about that. And what is
compulsory *in* living is this and that, the particular event, the
specific action, the peculiar disappointment. The history which
presses on the poet is not the history of historians but simply his
own; he feels griefs not grief; he meets men not man. Living is
not a cloudy gesture but a precise act. It is a kind of collision with
reality. Part of the equipment of any poet is a sense of human
reality better developed than in the rest of us. In Enright this is
a sense for the reality residing in, defined by, the exact and lucid
detail. We can see this sense operating in a remarkable early poem,
'The Chicken's Foot',[8] of which this is the second part:

At the end of this little street, unnamed, unfamed, a street
    that one might take
Unseeingly, to cheat the wind or to avoid one's friends,
A street like others, unduly ravaged by the tempest's tail,
Vulnerable to nature's riots though inured to man's –
At the bottom of this fluttered street, flat in the choked gutter,
I saw the neat claws, the precise foot, of a chicken –
Bright yellow leggings, precious lucid nails, washed by the waters,
Victim of our bellies, memorable sermon, oh murdered singing throat,
Confronting the battered traveller, fingers spread in admonition.

The wind howled louder in derision: oh literary pedestrian,
Small bankrupt moralist, oh scavenger of the obvious symbol!
But entering the huge house, where the wind's scattered voices,
Hot with insidious history, chill with foreboding, surged through my body,
The chicken's foot, naked and thin, still held my mind between its claws –
The cleanest thing, most innocent, most living, of that morning.

The run of this verse, combining an unimpeded movement
with a balanced disposition of phrase, recalls the manner of the
later Eliot. Eliot has clearly been a formative influence on
Enright's poetry, not an influence on imagery, tone or theme,

[8] *The Laughing Hyena.*

but a rhythmical one – the most intimate kind of influence one poet can have on another. Eliot's presence, however, is usually more absorbed, less distinct, than it is here. There is, I am sure, a reason for the insistence with which the poet calls attention to it in this poem. 'The Chicken's Foot' is a markedly 'literary' poem. In one sense the chicken's foot lies 'flat in the choked gutter' at the end of a little street. But it is also somewhere else. The formal literary manner, the traditional regularity of alliteration, the memory of Eliot, the reference to Chaucer, all set up an elaborate literary background wholly at odds with the humble bit of rubbish – a tessellated pavement on which the shocking, severed thing is flung. It is this, gleaming brilliantly against a pile of abstractions, which is 'The cleanest thing, most innocent, most living, of that morning' and this which holds not only the poet's but the reader's mind between its claws. And how vividly the reader heeds these ridiculously but impressively admonitory fingers. 'Heeding' is a very heightened form of observation. It takes a poet's power to tighten our slack vision into this intense activity, a poet's perceptiveness to turn the chicken's foot (or any object) from what it customarily is, a dim centre surrounded by 'a foggy sphere of influence', into

> ... the neat claws, the precise foot, of a chicken –
> Bright yellow leggings, precious lucid nails ...

By the end of the poem the chicken's foot has been invested with a clear Chaucerian pathos, unmuddied by sentimentality in a context which invites it. One check on sentimentality – often a fault of muzziness and incomplete realisation – is the firm definition of the object, the cleanliness of its outline. It is given an existence and a dignity of its own. A second check is the mockery aimed at the poet himself for finding so much significance in so commonplace a thing. One sees how the derisory phrases, 'literary pedestrian', 'bankrupt moralist', 'scavenger of the obvious symbol', while they deflate the poet, also suggest something about morals and symbols. Perhaps they too are rubbishy and defeated, victims of our souls instead of our bellies.

The effectiveness of 'The Chicken's Foot' depends, as with many of Enright's poems, on the exact defining of the central symbol. It is this which the poet, recognising its importance in his art, calls in another poem: 'The point of repose in the picture, the point of movement in us.' Enright's method, designed to fix this point accurately, is a discipline of clarity. It is a discipline which is averse to the attractions – the warm attractions – of the irrational. Enright wants his verse to move in a lucid, sensible air, not because he is in any way ignorant of hidden depths and subterranean disasters, but because he chooses to inhabit a clearer, Chaucerian universe. With such a care for clarity, so personal a bias towards light and intelligibility, the poet is bound to be troubled not only by 'the darkness of words', 'sinister symbols under ruin's shadow',[9] but by their ordinary duplicities. There is always in words a reluctance to be persuaded into coherence, and every poet has to struggle with this recalcitrance. Words are stubborn. They are today, even more than before, blandly evasive, ambiguous and sly. A contemporary poet has also to contend with something like a moral degeneracy in the words he uses. And yet it is from these elements, refractory, devious and dishonest, that the poet has to compose a structure of genuine feelings. No wonder that the poet recommends in 'A Desert Cure'[10] a regime of austerity for words.

Now is the time to take and know them – words – go with them
All the way, till the gasping tram sinks to its knees
In the open desert, devoid of palm-tree, or mirage, for refuge –
Only the dry donkey to receive you, and the stinging dust.

Or trap them in the stony customs shed: rap their dishonest hands
That slide towards false papers, or proffer folded notes in coveted
    currencies.
Do not spare: for elsewhere they would tear you:
Barbs in an enemy's watching mouth, claws on a friend's blind tongue,
The morning snake that creeps beneath the door.

Why is truth naked? Look at the long robes, sacred
Caftan and gallabieh, English suiting, committee-man in ties and devil's
    tails.
Lies dress the best. Leave them to die there – words –
On the verge of meaning, or purge in the open desert:
Shaken by the silent wind, shattered by the speechless sand.

One can see how the poet repelled by the dishonesty of words might want in the end to leave them there, to bleach in the open desert 'on the verge of meaning'. But he might instead turn back to the beginning, to words which are also on the verge of meaning – in the mouths of children. During those few years when a child

---

[9] 'Life and Letters', in *The Laughing Hyena*.
[10] *The Laughing Hyena*.

has come to feel at ease with words but is not yet expert in the hypocrisy of cliché, he uses language with an awkward and un-prompted honesty, as something original and alive. In a world where language moves between the poles of the committee and the advertisement, this gives an attentive listener, like this poet, the opportunity, as rewarding as it is rare, to hear language stirring into life. He can attend, as in a miniature play, to language per-forming the strange unpredictable motions of assuming new life. He can see, illustrated outside himself, the actions that words go through in his own mind. There are a number of poems, for example, 'Blue Umbrellas', 'First Death', 'End of a Hot Day', in which Enright makes the wayward, disconcertingly apt comment of a child the centre of a poem, disposing the poem round it or allowing it to grow from the child's words with skilled and gentle restraint. 'Blue Umbrellas'[11] takes off from one of those childish remarks which are, as it were, sideways to reality yet in some odd way also faithful to it:

'The thing that makes a blue umbrella with its tail –
How do you call it?' you ask. Poorly and pale
Comes my answer. For all I can call it is peacock.

Now that you go to school, you will learn how we call all sorts of things;
How we mar great works by our mean recital.
You will learn, for instance, that Head Monster is not the gentleman's
    accepted title;
The blue-tailed eccentrics will be merely peacocks;
    the dead bird will no longer doze
Off till tomorrow's lark, for the letter has killed him.
The dictionary is opening, the gay umbrellas close.

These words convey – with a fine economy and with regret that is also an unsentimental acceptance of the inevitable – a sense of that passage in a child's life from the time when his words are still marked by the bite of particularity to the time when they present the smooth undifferentiated surface of adult formulae. This passage isn't simply to be identified with the movement from language which is wholly concrete to language which is com-pletely abstract. The smallest child, using the simplest words, is performing a remarkably abstract and theoretic act, and the con-ventional adult using the most fatigued language still keeps some faint contact with the concrete. But the young child uses language in an active, discovering way, and not, as he will later, as an

[11] *Bread rather than Blossoms.*

instrument with which to attach general labels to passive experiences. With the young child – as with the poet – there is a bracing of energy between word and thought, a tension between word and thing. Even his oddest failures, his queerest gaffes, although as description they may be formally irrelevant, still contain a fundamental relevance to life. The Head Monsters and the blue umbrellas, although they may fail to raise the common image, surprise us by communicating the primary attribute of Headmasters and peacocks – their peculiar, living identity. The child's terms, although they may lack the symmetry of convention, display the proportions of life.

What makes the child's use of language distinctive, and what makes it so attractive to the contemporary poet, is that children are among the few in a more and more highly conditioned society capable of giving an unlicensed comment or an unpredictable reply. This capacity of the child is, of course, to be attributed to lack of experience, and not acuity of insight. But its result, the things said and offered, exhibits characteristics of freshness and vitality almost wholly bleached out of the current language. For a short time the child's sayings, unworn by routine, not yet smoothed down into a featureless response, present a human awkwardness and spontaneity rare enough to deserve a poet's attention. The child's words simply do not fit in; and in our world that is as good as a high degree of originality.

Dealing with a child's experience raises at once for the writer a technical problem, the one indeed that engaged Henry James's interests in *What Maisie Knew*. The problem is clearly more pressing in fiction but it cannot be avoided even in poetry. James saw that one cannot leave the child's consciousness alone, confused and obscure as it must be, to register the theme. The writer must piece out the child's partial, discontinuous understanding with an adult commentary. He can do this explicitly by making adult elucidation an answer to, or a commentary upon, the child's experience and the whole is turned into a pattern of stimulus and response, or he can do it implicitly by remaining within the universe of the child and by using adult understanding to clarify and order all that is obscurely contained in the child's faintly glimmering comprehension. In 'End of a Hot Day' Enright uses the first method, in 'First Death' the second.

> At last we can look at the melted moon:
> The grass is cool like olives: the cicadas

Are almost tender. 'Here at least is peace,'
We are trusting, 'after the day's hot murders' –
When the cat slinks by, a bird in his mouth
    betrayed by the evening's truce.

The child runs for a box,
The small remains are buried under the oily light.
She is happy: 'He will sleep in the box all night,
And tomorrow push his head through, like the daffodil.'
We swallow her bitter pill.

Tomorrow will be hot again; she will forget
To wait for the stone to roll away, the green feather
    to sprout, the twisted beak to twitter.
Every age has its advantages, and every weather.
Shall I beat the cat who ate the bird who ate
    the worm who might have eaten me?

                      ('End of a Hot Day')[12]

The crisp language and the muted imagery of taste recall by contrast the day's brutal heat, and make the treachery of the cat, like death itself, both natural and shocking. The child's remark, so pretty and fantastic, points up the savagery and hopelessness of the hot day. And yet her charmingly irrelevant words are an element in the situation – one of the advantages of her age and this weather – and deserve, as much as the bird's death, to be acknowledged, if the experience is to be fully rendered. Accepting the complexity of the concrete is what the poet is doing here and what he is justifying in the whip of the nursery-rhyme conclusion:

    Shall I beat the cat who ate the bird who ate
        the worm who might have eaten me?

I should not want to suggest that this poem was of more than minor interest, or that it was, even within its limits, completely successful. There is, for example, a slight loss of focus, and of propriety, in the phrase, 'she will forget/To wait for the stone to roll away'. No qualification of this sort, however, can be urged against 'First Death',[13] a brilliant evocation of the fundamental experience in a child's life, its first shattering meeting with human death:

    It is terrible and wonderful: we wake in the strange night
    And there is one bed empty and one room full: tears fall,
    The children comfort each other, hugging their knees,
        for what will the future be now, poor things?

[12] *Ibid.*   [13] *The Laughing Hyena.*

And next day there is no school, and meals are disorderly,
Things bought from shops, not the old familiar dishes.
New uncles come from far away, soft-voiced strangers
Drinking extraordinary wines. A kind of abstract kindliness
Fills the house, and a smell of flowers. Impossible to be bad –

Other nights pass, under conceded night-lights and a cloud
Of questions: shall we ever go back to school? Ever again
Go to the pictures? Are we too poor for new shoes?
                              Must we move
To a council house? Will any of our friends remember us?
Will it always be kind and quiet and sad, like this?

Uncles depart. We go for a week to a country aunt,
Then take a lodger. New shoes are bought – Oh, so this is the future!
How long will it last, this time? Never feel safe now.

One cannot but be impressed by the delicate rightness of tone in a poem where it would be only too easy to slide into the portentous and sentimental. It is a success, it seems to me, which depends on a set of exact, supple and beautifully maintained balances. For example, there is the nice equilibrium between general reflection and tight defining detail, between 'It is terrible and wonderful' and 'hugging their knees', or between 'A kind of abstract kindliness' and 'a smell of flowers'. Then there is the proportion between the new, impersonal atmosphere and the nagging questions which worry the children: on the one hand new uncles, soft-voiced strangers, extraordinary wines, on the other

> . . . shall we ever go back to school? Ever again
> Go to the pictures? Are we too poor for new shoes?
>   Must we move
> To a council house? Will any of our friends remember us?
> Will it always be kind and quiet and sad, like this?

If the tone does not sag, if the feeling does not loosen, that is because of the buoyancy and lightness of the rhythm which carries them, and which is itself a balance of phrases contrasted in weight and length, at one point unfolding slowly and easily, at another shutting down with abrupt finality. One can see too how the structure of the whole poem (which is pretty well repeated in the structure of each stanza) balances two distinct elements of the experience one against the other, the tremors of the children's disturbed present against premonitions about the future. The total effect of the poem is to bring home to the reader the children's suspicions – and then their terrified realisation – that the future is no simple flowering of a fragrant present, but the intrusion into their lives of a dangerous, treacherous force. Against its unpredictable and brutal workings they can offer only the sense of their powerlessness. 'Never feel safe now.'

So that the child in Enright's poetry is doubly significant. His capacity for the unrehearsed reply in a merely echoing world makes him significant *because* he is unrepresentative. But the child in another way faithfully represents the common run of men – those to whom Enright is most intimately drawn – because he is, like them, and more than most of them – the victim of power. It is the ultimate powerlessness which is communicated so directly in 'First Death', a sense not just of the inevitability of death, whether another's or one's own, but of the shattering of certainties and stabilities so that one must from now on hold oneself and one's beliefs tentatively and flinchingly. And it is powerlessness of this kind – bitterly acknowledged but also shruggingly accepted – which marks the figures thronging Enright's poetic world – the noodle-vendor, the trishaw driver, the one-eyed boy, the aged woman, 'the pimpled students in their costive dress', the girl in the bush:

> Perfect for the part, perfect,
> Except for the dropsy
> Which comes from polished rice.
> ('A Polished Performance')[14]

or Kazuo Yamamoto who found rat poison cheaper than aspirin, and Akiko San, the dumpy-legged, worried prostitute.

From the many sketches of these people – quick scrawls flicked down on any available paper – the reader gradually gets a view of the humanity that the poet sees. It is a view which is Oriental in its setting but Western in its sardonic precision – and I am not sure that it isn't universal in its truth. At its centre lies the recognition of the powerlessness of men. But perhaps, it seems to be suggested too, powerlessness isn't simply deprivation. It may also be the state of having not only necessities but illusions scraped away, and above all the illusion of power. The concomitant of powerlessness is a bitter sense of reality. The poor, the poet notes, wake up quickly. The poor, the appalling Eastern poor, are men reduced absolutely to their elements, men stripped of everything but a

---

[14] *Some Men are Brothers.*

residual human nature. All they own is a human identity but that is positive and incorruptible. In their indifference and passivity they have the look of statues, of statues hardly carved at all and barely to be recognised as human by an eye accustomed to more opulent outlines. But they also have the continuing resistance of stone. In 'Rice Coming Into Town'[15] it is this human nature which is deeply implicit in the details, this mere odour of humanity which is contrasted with sophisticated man:

> The barge lies low along the river,
> Deep in rice.
> Silent statues at its prow and stern
> (Dreaming old ballads of blood and gold?)
> Watch their images dissolve
>   into that foreign life.
> Those whom power has not yet
>   tended to corrupt
> (Beyond the common power
> To grow a crop or mildly cheat a neighbour).
>
> They watch their silent images
>   melt into the water:
> As they melt – so it seems –
> Into a gorging town, a coup d'état,
> A street of ministries, of restaurants,
> A smell of jasmine, opium, petrol,
> A brace of schools, a pack of characteristics,
> A voice heard in the councils of the world.
>
> Statues, too tired to talk?
>   Too wise? Too ignorant?
> (Dreaming new thoughts of blood and gold?)
> Will power ever manage to corrupt
>   (even tend to)
> All of these?
>   How much power is there in this world?

Upon such scenes as these, and on their merely human occupants, the poet turns a gaze which is accurate, tender and sceptical – a characteristic blend of qualities. The accuracy is in the notation, the tenderness is for the object, the scepticism is for himself. After all the poet-observer has the privilege of not enduring what those he watches suffer. And isn't there a pretension, a degree of conceit, in translating human suffering so directly into art, as he hints in an untitled poem in *Some Men are Brothers*?

[15] *Ibid.*

Simply, he was human, did no harm, and suffered for it.
His name? – We might be tempted by its liquid vowel sounds,
   the richness of its rhythms –

I've said too much already.
      Writers of epitaphs, in your conceit, remember:
There may be relatives still living.

Scepticism may be too hard, too intellectual a word for the wry, deflationary attitude which we feel to be so distinctly a modern mood. (Not that in Enright's writing we are ever unaware of the movement of an athletic intelligence.) Scepticism as it appears here is a preference for the bone of actuality and a distaste for the obesity of cliché, whether moral or intellectual. And it isn't with Enright simply negative or just tediously clever. It takes its stand – I mustn't be diffident about using such terms of a writer who is fundamentally serious – on a metaphysic, a view of man, and a morality, the morality of a common human nature. The view of man which stresses his uniqueness, and the morality which insists on his unity, show themselves in a nice balance in the tiny poem, 'Man':[16]

We should treasure this cobra
Were it the only one.
Can't Nature take the human hint,
Must we help her on?

Soul, then morals, tried and failed.
If this fails too, there's only tooth and claw.
Yet brothers are exhausting, row on row:
Give me a friend – he murmured – three or four,

Who know all men are brothers, even though
They may not like their brothers saying so.

The metaphysic gets its urgency from a prevailing sense of the special precariousness of modern existence – life lived along a precipice; the morality gets its strength from the poet's exact, accurate understanding of his own feelings. There is nothing gusty or Whitmanesque in his 'all men are brothers' since he doesn't attempt to hide that 'brothers are exhausting, row on row'. What is so characteristic of Enright, as of today, is that serious views are held so flippantly. To Enright it is quite natural (though on occasion, perhaps, only irresistible) for the poet as clown to see life as

[16] *Ibid.*

a farce. And few of us I fancy – and certainly not the young – will find the conditions of modern life such as to make this notion of its absurdity inexplicable. To Enright there is little difference between practising an art and acting the monkey or between honouring the muse and taking the mickey – at the expense of himself as well as of others.

> Once again the Year of the Monkey is here.
> I was born in the Year of the Monkey –
> Surely a fellow can talk about himself a bit,
>   in his own year?
>
> Monkeys are like poets – more than human.
> Which is why they do not take us very seriously.
> Not to be taken seriously is rather painful.
>   To a corner of my cage I retired, mysteriously,
> And had sad thoughts. (They may have been deep.)
> Big eyes damp with a semi-permanent tear, my thin hands
>   held my heavy head from tumbling into sleep.
>
>   ('Monkey')[17]

There is a sharp discrepancy, of which the poet is well aware, between this comedian's manner and the subjects which a poet with so distinctly contemporary a sensibility is bound to treat – which itself may be part of what makes him so much of the moment. 'Stop that clowning at once if not sooner'[18] is a poem which makes this contrast explicit:

> Giggling on the edge of a precipice –
> Shameful! They'll think you haven't noticed it.
> Or worse, that you're the sort of person
>   for whom abysses don't exist,
> Being one coarse-grained vacant space yourself. . .
>
> For the time needs –
>   stop giggling on the brink of precipices
> While I'm talking to you! –
>   heavyweight intellects, sober serious men.
>
>   'Unfortunately it gets them,'
> Giggling on the verge of nothing.
> 'Here's a profound hole, yet no deeper than a coffin.'
> Hoping that not too many (even that he may not)
>   fall into it,
> Wagging his arms and legs, and hoping. . .

Hope – smaller and greyer than optimism – is one of the homely

[17] *Ibid.*   [18] *Ibid.*

35

clutch of qualities (a modest decency, a mild charity, an un-emphatic tolerance) celebrated in this verse. These unpretentious, appealing virtues, as human as a hiccup and as common, preserve the human idiom in a context full of violence and terror. And that after all is what good poems like good acts (which, the poet points out, *are* achieved though seldom by oneself) try to do – to make audible the inflections of a human voice in conditions in which it may be suffocated by mechanisation in a long twilight or annihi-lated by politics in a flash. It is this voice, mostly offhand, occasionally intense, at other times sly, glum, comic, irritable but always real, which is the true subject as well as the natural medium of a poetry trying above all to construct and preserve a human idiom, and to defend and praise the validity of private experience. In 'The Monuments of Hiroshima'[19] the poet makes the point by exposing the contrast which exists between even the diminished vitality of common, silly obituary phrases and the ghastly lan-guage and results of State action:

> The roughly estimated ones, who do not sort well
>   with our common phrases,
> Who are by no means eating roots of dandelion,
>   or pushing up the daisies.

> The more or less anonymous, to whom no human idiom
>   can apply,
> Who neither passed away, or on,
>   nor went before, nor vanished on a sigh.

> Little of peace for them to rest in, less of them
>   to rest in peace:
> Dust to dust a swift transition, ashes to ash
>   with awful ease.

> Their only monument will be of others' casting –
> A Tower of Peace, a Hall of Peace, a Bridge of Peace
>   – who might have wished for something lasting,
> Like a wooden box.

Poetic intentions of this kind are natural to one who believes that 'civilisation consists in the diminution of human tears' and who prefers the paddy-fields where the ancient woman spoons its ration of hot harsh food to each rice plant, or a tram-ride through the ancient capital to 'the cafés where the cultured pique and pine' or 'the largish whitish newish building. . .devoted to the

[19] *Bread rather than Blossoms.*

study of the Liberal Arts and Humanities'. Enright, clearly, feels more at home with the humble tom-fool than with 'polished Monsieur Angst'. Many – more as he develops – of his poems appear to be written in opposition. Very few express the unflurried simplicity of a single, total experience. In this sense these poems are impure. They tend more and more to be harassed by disagreement and protest. Even in a poem called 'The Peaceful Island',[20] which is about a day spent away from the city, its vices and charlatan voices, in a place where

> The islanders' speech is soft and slow:
> No aids to their dialect have yet been printed;
> It sounds like the surge of the sea on powdery sands;
> It is empty of oaths. . .

we find the poet, dizzy with lack of sleep, passing the time by throwing stones at bottles, which represent a procurer, a flinty industrialist, a well-known poet and an expert in traditions. On occasion even, the poet-observer becomes the poet-demonstrator and the poem a cross gesticulation or a yelp of anger. But more often his antagonism is cool and directed. It is turned, as you would expect from one who is above all on the side of what is real, however sleazy its form, against frauds and cryptos, the conmen of the intellect: against the superior person ('the gentleman of spiritual truths'), 'grave intellectuals doing their strip-tease', politicians –

> The only enigma that I saw
> Was the plump sayings of the politicians
> Against the thin faces of the poor. . .
> ('Oriental Politics')[21]

against critics, who dig for the profound, and scholars (choosing a glittering fragment of Zen, or the cracked semblance of an Emblem. . .).

If I have been using terms like hostility, conflict, protest, antagonism, this has been in an effort to acknowledge a characteristic quality of Enright's poetry – that it is so honestly, so acutely personal. In these poems the poetry is of the person and the person is in the poetry. Which poses the question: what portrait – or since Enright works with light fleeting touches – what sketch of this person begins at length to appear? It seems to be that of someone who sees himself as small, unsuccessful and shabby, a half-

[20] *Some Men are Brothers.*   [21] *Bread rather than Blossoms.*

37

deserving, half-predestined victim, the opposite of the big, booming canary in the cage who is:

> – Florid, complacent, rent-free and over-fed,
> Feather-bedded, pensioned, free from wear and tear.
> ('Displaced Person Looks at a Cage-Bird')[22]

Not, it is clear, the central man, who presumably belongs to and
unites both wings, but the wretched man in the middle like the
lowest member of the great tribe of Wang:

> As the evening dies, their thoughts incline towards both,
> neither quite present, neither quite absent.
> Would you call this exile? It seems like what life is.
>
> ('Exile?')[23]

The model of this person is not 'the noble poet with his noble
theme, *contemporain de jours prodigieux*', but the Egyptian
student in Birmingham or the Japanese dancing girl or the work-
man grumbling mildly over his wage – people who don't know it
all, who in a world tending to abolish it keep alive the old human
habit of *naïveté*.

> Take solace where you find it. In your gardener, say –
> For bed and board, he chops the jungle from your square of lawn.
> Perhaps he'll keep the queer old habit just alive...
>
> ('Words Without Songs')[24]

Or perhaps he won't. Perhaps the jungle will choke the lawn.

Such is the *persona* of the observer in these poems of observation; and since there is in human nature an irresistible tendency
to assimilate the seen to the seer (a tendency which becomes in
the tension of art what Coleridge called a coincidence of subject and object), we find that for Enright the central, the
establishing figure in life, is someone like this too. His representative character is the private man, the cheerful, stricken
occupant of the middle air. He is the one with a hankering for
health, physical and moral, who is just the same riddled by
ordinary diseases and common faults. He suffers the usual suffer-
ings in the usual way: he complains and puts up with them. He is
neither innocent nor knowing. His standards have slipped a bit,
but on the other hand he has broadened his acquaintance with the
style of human beings. This is someone I can recognise – and
not merely from looking outwards. His outline, his wrinkles and

[22] *Some Men are Brothers.*   [23] *Ibid.*   [24] *Ibid.*

voice are all familiar and cherished. His existence, which these
poems movingly evoke and confirm, is proof, a demonstration in
today's words, of the survival, patient and resolute, of a common
human being.

> Was Freud entirely right? We rise to chase those inner phantoms,
> Who often end by chasing us. The sleeping dogs
> Start up from every corner: they have not read the textbooks
> That bid us pat their heads. The only bone they want is us...
>
> Was Goethe wholly wrong? It is by onward striding
> We lay our ghosts, he said. Seeking neither to avoid nor meet.
> No tree stays small through fear of meeting lightning:
> The strawberry finds its ripeness in the straw.
>   They grow, or rest,
> In light or darkness. Doing what they have to do,
> And suffering what, and only what, they must.
>   ('Baie des Anges, Nice')[25]

[25] *The Laughing Hyena.*

3
CRITICISM

Enright has practised the craft of literary criticism almost as long as he has the art of poetry. His first prose work, *The World of Dew* (1955), a study of Japanese life and sensibility, shows in the appropriate places critical acumen of an uncommon kind. He has published three collections of critical essays, his method lending itself to the particularised experience of a given work and a highly specified commentary on it, so that he uses a sprinter's nerves rather than a long-distance runner's stamina in *The Apothecary's Shop* (1957), *Conspirators and Poets* (1966), *Man is an Onion* (1972). In addition he is the co-editor with Takamichi Ninomiya of an anthology of contemporary Japanese poetry, *The Poetry of Living Japan* (1957) and, with Ernst de Chickera, an edition of *English Critical Texts* (1962), both of them prefaced by concise and pointed introductions. He is also the author of a work on Shakespeare, *Shakespeare and the Students* (1970), a study of *King Lear*, *Anthony and Cleopatra*, *Macbeth* and *The Winter's Tale*. If in his *persona* as poet one thinks of Enright as the poet of humanism and light, in his character as critic he appears as the critic of human feeling and untethered intellect, or since this phrase suggests a certain goatlike capering, perhaps I should say of the free intelligence, except that that again carries with it intimations of the booming mock-modesty of the fashionable thinker. Enright, on the other hand, is truly modest but also remarkably assured, a combination as original in his criticism as the temperament exhibited in his poetry, which blends much gentleness of response with a sharply sardonic vision. In a glum, extreme world criticism manifesting such gaiety of spirit and moral feeling is indeed comforting and reviving.

One cannot help but be struck by Enright's critical range. If he is a sprinter he has performed on tracks round the world. If he works by concentration in the review rather than the extended essay, the intensities of the various pieces make up into an unusually wide scope. He has written on Ben Jonson and Philip

Massinger on the one hand, on Rilke and Thomas Mann on the other; on the 1914–18 war poets and especially on Wilfred Owen, on Goethe and D. H. Lawrence, on Shakespeare and C. P. Cavafy, on Franz Werfel and Italo Svevo, on Virginia Woolf and E. M. Forster, and on writers as different as Mary McCarthy, Lawrence Durrell, Philip Larkin, Dylan Thomas, Cyril Connolly and Robert Graves, T. S. Eliot and F. R. Leavis. Nor has he neglected to address himself to more general critical problems like the achievement of *Scrutiny* or the rise of the criticocracy or the significance of belief in criticism or the meaning of tradition in literature. Each particular response has that braced and living quality which comes from an unfatigued, vividly personal reaction – no peering at the thing through the fly-spotted muslin of other critics' views; the whole scope of the work has implicit in it the unity of a temperament. The body of Enright's critical writing is supported by a considerable weight of learning, unpretentious learning completely incorporated into the stuff of the critic and not carried about like lumber cracking a bent back.

As I think my account has shown, Enright's misfortunes in public life, and there have been a number of them (he quotes[1] Heine's advice to his descendants, 'to be born with thick skins on their backs'), came mostly from acting in an ordinary human way in official situations. And as I have just said, his poetry and his criticism manifest at every point a peculiarly human tone. Since of Enright we can say what Henry James said of his father, 'his philosophy was in his tone', I want to fill out what I mean by looking in turn at his criticism of Shakespeare; of German writers; of some contemporary writers; and, finally, at his treatment of certain more general critical problems.

Enright's attitude to Shakespeare is an unusual one among critics, i.e. gratitude. He is, in consequence, opposed both to those who niggle and carp in the hunt for faults in an ingenious though graceless way, as well as those who having rescued us from the smoke and fire of romanticism now drop us 'into the hygienic incinerators of symbolism, imagery-computation, a curiously trite moralising, and philosophising of a sort so primitive as undoubtedly to have contributed to the discredit which literature has fallen into among the serious-minded'.[2] For Enright the plays are plays, the poetic, that is the most powerful, recreation of human

[1] *Memoirs of a Mendicant Professor*, epigraph.
[2] *Shakespeare and the Students*, p. 10.

conduct, and in his crisp and feeling commentaries he resists the current tendency to dissolve them into clouds of theory or psychiatry or to indulge in the game of splitting up dramatic actions into knots and trains of symbols. Instead of breaking up the object into its constituent elements, Enright brings to bear the whole of himself, a complex of sympathies, prejudices, personal history, a set of fundamental human and untechnical standards and assumptions, a supple intelligence and a deflationary wit, and allows all that to lock in an energetic embrace with the play. The resulting commentary, concise as it invariably is, and intensely personal, has the unusual completeness of a full human reaction.

The early essay on *Coriolanus* in *The Apothecary's Shop* is a characteristic critical exercise, immediate in its response and mixing moral sanity and sensitive charitableness in its judgements. A cool eye marks off the essential data, categorising the politics of the city and the militarism of the hero. Coriolanus, as Enright sees him, is a hero, certainly, but a military hero not a tragic hero. 'Coriolanus in a tight corner is an awe-inspiring spectacle and there, while it lasts, he is really alive: a hero is the thing he is best at being.' But there is nothing in him, no gift or talent, relevant to a position other than that of wartime general: 'If only, we may feel, he could be rather more introspective – in the way that Macbeth is – rather more conscious of the cries of his lawful victims! If only we were persuaded that there is more to him than is reflected in his armour.' *Coriolanus* is a play in which all the powerful characters throw their weight against life or against the kind of love which Virgilia stands up for. The universe of the play is that of politics and the Rome we see in the play is a hard city, in which the inhabitants form parties rather than relationships. It gives a final impression of aridness and waste and it explores the dangers of a situation in which each opposing side understands the other but neither side understands itself. In *Memoirs of a Mendicant Professor* Enright speaks of the dry territory where politics flourish. It is a desert gradually extending its sway. But, he says, 'there is a remote region in the soul to which politicians have not yet managed to secure unfailing access, and people do have an inkling that there is something better to be had, something wiser, something older, which politics can interpret, perhaps use or abuse, but not replace'.[3] *Coriolanus* is a play which offers us no guide to that remote region.

[3] *Memoirs*, p. 186.

Whereas *King Lear, Anthony and Cleopatra, Macbeth,* and *The Winter's Tale,* plays which Enright chooses to explicate scene by scene in his book on Shakespeare,[4] penetrate deeply into that territory. Enright's work on Shakespeare springs from a double intention. The first, and expressed, intention is that a running commentary on a play is so rebarbative and unseductive that even the student most susceptible to the influence of the critic rather than of the playwright will be driven back to the text. The other implicit intention which animates the whole treatment is to stress the human rather than the mythical or the divine in Shakespeare's characters, and above all in Shakespeare's heroes. If the limitation of Enright's treatment is to underemphasise the magnificent and terrible in the characters, as it does the gorgeousness of the rhetoric, its advantage is to stress the reality, sometimes the quite homely and freckled reality, of the characters. How human Lear appears when he is seen as one 'proposing to give up something which he is apparently fairly good at – ruling a pre-historic Britain – for something which indeed he has taken too little care of'. Anthony is pictured as a 'professional strong-man, bursting out of his breastplate like a circus performer' even more than the triple pillar of the world; Cleopatra exhibits jealousy of the legal wife, the married woman, and 'then brings up the old reproach that since her lover has been untrue to his wife, it is all too likely that he will be untrue to his mistress as well'. Her sentiments if godlike in language are still woman-like in trend. Of Macbeth he says that one of the teacher's concerns will be 'to save Macbeth from shrinking under the influence of metaphysical magic into a poor little man (whose clothes do not fit!), henpecked by his wife, by the Weird Sisters, and by Evil Absolute and Disembodied'. Macbeth and Lady Macbeth display two different conceptions of what it is to be a man. Macbeth contends that one can be a man only up to a certain point, thereafter one becomes not a man but a beast; Lady Macbeth's view is that a man ought to be more and more a man and the more outrageous he becomes the closer he gets to the ideal, 'She has no inkling of those limits set upon humanity' which so exercise Macbeth. Lady Macbeth's ferocious and unfeminine outbursts oddly accentuate the fact that she is and remains a woman. She and Macbeth, as Bradley says, are 'born to rule, if not to reign', 'and the tragedy of Macbeth is, of course, that he is exactly fitted by nature for the throne, but

4 *Shakespeare and the Students.*

he can only obtain the throne by means which exactly unfit him for it'. The jealousy of Leontes in *The Winter's Tale*, a play which is 'more tragedy than comedy, more realism than romance', follows logically upon the yielding of Polixenes, as Coleridge noted. The jealousy, that is, begins in a natural way and its delineation is authentic and complete, 'compelling almost to the point of nausea, and quite impervious to the most assiduous symbolists'. So that Enright's treatment, here and elsewhere, is concerned not with elements, doctrines, themes or metaphysical absolutes, but with the infinitely more complicated variety, the almost drunken manifoldness of human relations and human personality.

Perhaps Enright's sympathy is most lively, his method most profitable, when he considers characters of the second range, Cordelia, or Edgar, or Edmund. It may be because they are more contained, more human, more open to his alert psychological perception. Cordelia, for instance, in her incapacity to heave her heart into her mouth, reveals herself, in Enright's phrase, 'a true Englishman'; Edgar stays 'paralysed in his banal and egotistical little moralisings'. But the most illuminating of all is the note on Edmund which I should like to quote to show the characteristic tone, the capacity to define, and the linguistic vivacity:

'Thou, Nature, art my goddess...' The historical critics, quickly shuffling into their smelly doublets and hose, have put Edmund in his place before he appears – or just as soon as he appears. 'No medieval devil ever bounced on the stage with a more scandalous self-announcement', says John F. Danby.[5] This, I take it, means that although Edmund speaks a lot of good modern sense, we ought to feel obliged to ignore much of what he says, and hence to discount the energy, the life, the ingenuity in him – which, alas, is all the more striking for the poor show Edgar puts up much of the time. 'Now, gods, stand up for bastards!' Perhaps they don't, as the play turns out, or not less ambiguously than they stand up for anyone else. But it seems to me that Shakespeare stands up for this particular bastard, who has had an unlucky start in life: unlike Regan and Goneril, the women who pull him down with their love as they pull their father down with their lack of love. Scandalous? It is a splendid speech and all the history in the world won't persuade us at this point that 'Nature' is such a reprehensible concept by comparison with 'custom' or the mere 'curiosity of nations'. Says Edmund, 'Fine word, "legitimate"!' We are to suffer so many dreary fine words from his legitimate brother.[6]

The life of Shakespeare's characters in Enright's interpreta-

[5] *Shakespeare's Doctrine of Nature*, London 1949.
[6] *Shakespeare and the Students*, p. 25.

tion may not be lived, to quote his poem 'The Noodle-Vendor's Flute' again,

In real cities, real houses, real time.

Nevertheless, the point of their existence, and of the poetry which evokes it, is precisely to illumine the existence of those who do. As we should expect of a writer who is a poet as well as a critic, in fact more of a poet than a critic, Enright does not exaggerate the realism of the real, but he does see the purpose of art, above all perhaps of dramatic art, as extending our experience of reality. In a nicely balanced essay, 'Poetic Satire and Satire in Verse: A Consideration of Ben Jonson and Philip Massinger',[7] Enright, with this kind of distinction in mind, contrasts the poetic satire of Jonson with Massinger's satire in verse. The packed power of the poetry in Jonson's play creates both the character of Volpone, and simultaneously a 'counter-Volpone' by virtue of which the corruption of the first Volpone is magnificently defined and judged. Philip Massinger, on the other hand, with his nervous predilection for a minutely accurate realism, displays a lack of faith in metaphorical expression, in poetry itself. He is working towards a different conception of drama in which the word is to wield less power than it did in Jonson. With Jonson we have the depth of reality poetry produces; with Massinger the surface satire of prose. Jonson, that is, uses fundamentally the same means for the same ends, as Shakespeare; Massinger, distrusting metaphor, suspicious of the poetic mode itself, anticipates the cooler, less creative drama of prose and the Restoration.

If I say that Enright's attitude to Shakespeare and the Elizabethans for all its freshness (both in spontaneity and indeed cheek), and for all its disconcerting ability to jolt us out of routine, is not unexpected, I am not, I realise, saying anything particularly pointed or informative, except perhaps to suggest that there is in Enright, sustaining the flippancy, a kind of orthodoxy or centrality or sanity of taste and judgement. On the other hand, given his temperament and the nature of the material, I *am* surprised at his very positive feelings for German literature. In an entertaining flight, 'Aimez-vous Goethe',[8] Enright specifies the reasons why so many English readers are ill-disposed towards German literature. They find it – as indeed Matthew Arnold observed did most

[7] *The Apothecary's Shop*, pp. 54–74.
[8] *Conspirators and Poets*, pp. 208–18.

Englishmen in the nineteenth century – wordy, philosophical, humourless, both highly abstract and crammed with details, produced and populated by obtrusive authors, naïvely symbolic, and grossly mixed in its categories, mingling fantasy and realism, the elephantine tread and the faery footstep. It has not, particularly in the case of Goethe, been well served by translators, although translators have done far more for it than British critics and Germanists. (Not that German critics have been very helpful either. From his own experience of working in a German university, Enright came to understand that the literary critic, as distinct from the scholar, was a form of life only surpassed in frivolity and vulgarity by the creative writer.) It has to be added too, as Enright puts it, 'that in some cases non-admiration of German literature arises out of – or *is* – non-admiration of Germans'. 'Not all English non-likers of German literature non-like it', as Enright puts it, for all the reasons cited, but that the reasons are real, that is existing, can hardly be doubted. Perhaps no modern – or ancient – English critic has written with such justice and delicacy of German writers as Enright, and above all of his saints, Goethe and Thomas Mann.

Enright's view of Goethe, the genius of an enigmatic clarity, is developed most fully in an early essay on *Wilhelm Meister*, that ambiguous milksop. Lawrence, as Enright notes, was indignant about the novel. 'I think *Wilhelm Meister* is amazing as a book of peculiar immorality, the perversity of intellectualised sex, and the utter incapacity for any *development* of contact with any other human being which is peculiarly bourgeois and Goethian.' To this Enright's response is, 'But then we have to laugh: it is, after all, a comic novel, about the adventures of an over-read young intellectual, half in league with and half at war with the *Zeitgeist*.'[9] As a work of art the novel is a long way from perfect. It has no unity of plot or theme, its characters are often silly, Wilhelm's adventures frequently boring. 'True, Wilhelm has many lessons to learn; but it is hard that so often he should learn them at the reader's expense.'[10] Structurally the work is broken into two pieces, with the pietistic 'Confessions of a Beautiful Soul' clamped between. *Wilhelm Meister* is certainly not a popular novel; not even a great one. But it has a precarious unity, a strange note of ambiguity which eases the juxtaposition of the exquisite and the coarse, the feeling and the cynical, tragedy and farce. Its con-

[9] *The Apothecary's Shop*, p. 109. [10] *Ibid.* p. 101.

sistency is a continual changing of tone and the irony of which this is the expression. What appeals to Enright is that Goethe, who throughout the novel uses and abuses contemporary conventions, quite deliberately in the service of disabusing life of unreality, is powerfully against the whole symbolic approach to literary truth. He is so distrustful of symbolism that he wishes to bring art even closer to real life than is safe for it. Not that he belonged to the realist or documentary school: he merely thought that 'a rich manifold life, brought close to our eyes, would be enough without any expressed tendency which, after all, is only for the intellect'. His striving to include the totality of his experience in the novel makes him unsympathetic to a public tolerant about both romanticism and classicism so long as a clean distinction is made between them. Goethe does not take sides about theoretical ideas in the way we like to do now and so he isn't easily put into one category or the other. 'What is rarely perceived is that Goethe does take a side, that he does commit himself, and with a loving whole-heartedness that has become increasingly uncommon among writers. He accepts, above all other considerations, the prime value of being alive. . . It is the sin against life that is dreadful, not the sin against ideas: the scaffold might be necessary in Goethe's world, but the concentration camp would not exist.'[11] His quest was for some means of avoiding chaos in life and art without imposing any categorical law. His aspiration towards unity was limited by his sense of the manifold. Because he refuses to use symbolism only he employs an undisciplined quantity of characters themselves engaged in an unregimented variety of activities. In fact Goethe has tried to apply to the novel the very principle which *Wilhelm Meister's Apprenticeship* sets out to convey: 'that it is life itself, rich in action, not free from error, but uncluttered by the symbols of introspection or abstract thought, that counts'.[12]

If we still read Goethe, what would his name mean? Enright's answer would be a whole cast of mind shown most notably in a sense of balance and spiritual poise. It would include the capacity to examine perversion and to sympathise with disease while reporting on the one with a clean tongue and not exhorting to the other. It would contain the further capacity to be an artist among the bourgeois and by an agile twist a bourgeois among the artists. It would mean showing oneself at the same time a thorough

[11] *Ibid.* p. 93.　　[12] *Ibid.* p. 111.

German and a good European; and the ability 'to plunge into a cloud of metaphysical speculations and then to emerge as dry and precise as ever, bearing one or two clear and very human perceptions'.[13] This set of qualities, called up by the name of Goethe, itself calls up the name of Thomas Mann. The comedy of *The Magic Mountain*, the tragedy of *Doctor Faustus*, the farce of *The Confessions of Felix Krull*, are among the supreme contemporary vindications of the novel's potentialities as a form of high art. 'The final paradox is that, in spite of their apparent preoccupation with disease, they are full of athletic vigour and enthusiasm for things human. Unlike much of our most brilliant modern writing, they send us back into life, not terrified into despair or dullness or quiescence by the sight of others' follies, but cheerfully prepared to commit our own.'[14] We think of Mann, with some reason, as a novelist of general ideas and symbols. But he is not the novelist of abstract ideas or of point-to-point symbolism, $a = z$ and $b = y$. The reader is not confronted with any Philosophical Idea or any Psychological Study, but with views which cannot be disengaged from the person who delivers them and with attitudes that cannot be divorced from appearances, figures, history and individual reality. So that Mann works not with airy-fairy abstractions like the progressive, the reactionary, the humanist and the artist, but with such solid creations as Settembrini, Naphta, Serenus Zeitblom and Adrian Leverkühn. 'What we have in the end is *symbolism* in an uncomplicated but great sense of the word: an exact and lucid scene which at the same time gives definition to and takes definition from an exact and lucid idea.'[15] Just as Goethe is studded with maxims, set attitudes and stated theories of behaviour (ironically shown up in the end), so Mann is packed with long informative passages, with digressions, with circumstantial filling in of backgrounds and antecedents. Both Goethe and Mann eschew in the name of exhaustiveness any pronounced selectiveness or weighing of the scales. The work of each is massive and explicit. This is a kind of writing the English reader is generally ill-prepared for, just as he is for work in which there appear to be too many ideas, too diverse attitudes, too many minutely presented arguments. But what in the end Mann has achieved, Enright points out, is work which enforces the truth that a man's ideas are neither simply acquired from others nor simply self-inspired, but arise from the interaction of

[13] *Ibid.* p. 123.   [14] *Ibid.* p. 120.   [15] *Ibid.* p. 114.

inner and outer in the very process of living. 'There is truly speaking no such thing as "education for living", but only education through living; and no valid distinction can be drawn between "life" and "thought" or "life" and "spirit", if both are real.'[16] Mann, he says, and supremely *Doctor Faustus*, offers us,

hard, solid work which does not hesitate to be sometimes a little slow in order to be exhaustive, is not afraid of seriousness, despises fashion, prizes the detail to the profit of the planned whole, achieves what is usually left to poetry and achieves it without trying to be poetry and becoming poetic prose – work that ultimately draws its amazing energy from the author's fast hold on 'the anti-diabolic faith, that mankind has after all a "keen hearing", and that words born of one's own striving may do it good and not perish from its heart.'[17]

When Enright turns from Mann to lesser figures, Günter Grass, Uwe Johnson, Heinrich Böll, the generosity, the largeness of mind and spiritual respect induced in him by the genius of the greatest European novelist of the twentieth century, is sprinkled with a sceptical and characteristically astringent salt. Günter Grass, 'the Tristram Shandy of the age of Adenauer', applies something of Mann's meticulousness and exhaustiveness in the service of what often turns out to be a dirty joke or a slapstick anecdote. In his *Cat and Mouse* the parts are manipulated with loving care and there are moments of miraculous freshness and hallucinatory clarity; but the whole crumbles before one's eyes, and the action is repetitious, mystificatory or satirical in a slapdash way. Imprisoned in his corpulent third novel, *Dog Years*, a thinner, more considerable one is struggling to get out. The book is a powerful work with a stronger density of detail and documentation; and in spite of too many symbolic red-herrings, and an apparently deliberate blurring of the print, *Dog Years* is a novel of much energy and inventiveness which can – just – afford some 'major failures of form and uncertainty of intention'.

In *Local Anaesthetic*, in which toothache is the figure of human suffering and Chancellor Kiesinger's plump Germany is that of human society, the subject is essentially this: 'What does St George do when the local dragon is "relatively" not such a bad beast and the villagers are not especially terrorised by it?'[18] Grass's treatment of this theme is heavy-handed and repetitive, at times wastefully mystifying, but it is also conscientious and

[16] *Ibid.* p. 119.   [17] *Ibid.* p. 144.
[18] *Man is an Onion*, London 1972, p. 98.

balanced, offering no evidence that Grass is documenting the tragic bankruptcy of liberalism.

Uwe Johnson's *Speculations about Jakob* is 'a mystery with little cloak about it and no dagger at all', in a style consistently rebarbative, obscure and abstract, which could have been a very considerable novel had it only been readable. Henrich Böll's *The Clown* is one of the 'few novels coming out these days which aren't either a kind of syrup or a kind of emetic'. Böll has something to say. Unfortunately he says it several times, not understanding that to say it four times isn't four times as effective as saying it once. The German literary Renaissance, after Mann, is not, it seems, on the same level as the German economic miracle.

Take Hermann Hesse, for example. He was a good man who recognising very early the onset of Germany's Faustianity removed himself to single-souled Switzerland. Not all his fiction is Teutonically heavy and humourless, drunk with ideas, but a good deal of it is. 'It is not so much that Hesse dramatises or even popularises ideas as that he takes the stiffening out of them, sandpapers the sharper edges away, and hands them over to his readers to play with as they will. A highly cultivated person, he is the ideal second-order writer for the sort of serious-minded reader desirous to believe that he is grappling successfully with intellectual and artistic profundities of the first order.'[19]

A critic as practised and accomplished as Enright deals with major writers like Goethe or minor ones like Günter Grass or Böll, on their merits and on his terms – calmly, with the impartiality of the interested but disengaged, and with no more personal commitment than to the truth and relevance of what he says. But there are writers towards whom the critic may feel a special affinity springing from some proportion of temperament or common bias of sensibility. In these cases one gets from the critic, at least from this critic, not just an intelligent clarity of explication and analysis, not just the enlightenment of qualified approval or graduated dissent in his judgement, but also a more creative kind of insight and the more moving subtleties of sympathy which appear when a flow of fellow feeling moves unobstructed and at home among the distinctive complexities of the work in question. Two writers with whom Enright has such a relationship, who seem unusually accessible to his approach and

[19] *Ibid.* p. 73.

transparent to his sight, are C. P. Cavafy and Italo Svevo. In the course of discussing English translations of Cavafy Enright remarks, 'how health-giving, in this degenerate context, is the presence of a decadent poet!', the degenerate context being 'a noisy, virile, goody-goody and flaccid world'. Cavafy was sad, a bit of a cynic, something of an aristocrat, a connoisseur, an imperfect gentleman, 'It is not that Cavafy reminds us that we are merely human, he reminds us that we *are* human.' There is no tendency to corrupt in his poems which are no more likely to produce homosexuals than Yeats's love poems are to produce heterosexuals.

One sees particularly in Enright's remarks about Cavafy how vividly even the sympathetic critic, doing his best to submit himself to the author he is reading, to be detached and impartial, sees himself in the object of his criticism; and in this case, we must say, very justifiably sees himself, or someone very like himself. 'The combination of tenderness with irony, the cool confrontation of disaster, the gift of nimbly enlarging a specific historical incident into general applicability.'[20] How apt, how just, these words are, not to Cavafy alone but to Enright himself.

> Let the flippant call me flippant.
> In serious matters I have always been
> most diligent...
> ('A Byzantine Noble in Exile Writing Verses')[21]

Honesty, irony, tenderness, desperation, a firm morality, compassion for the unheroic living, a keen worm's-eye view of history: these are the marks of a poetry Enright feels intensely appealing and cogent. They are also those of Italo Svevo's three novels, *A Life*, *As A Man Grows Older*, and *Confessions of Zeno*. The first is a sad uncomplicated story of a poor fish, whose suicide seems, at least to his creator, the one successful act of his life; *As A Man Grows Older* can make plain the mediocrity of Emilio, another poor fish, without the least trace of a sneer, and it is written with the same quiet clarity and decency as *A Life*; in *Confessions of Zeno*, however, the poor fish not only survives, he triumphs – gets away, in fact. Zeno satirises the physical sickness and enervation of Svevo's heroes. 'Continually beset by mysterious aches and pains, he lives on avidly while stronger characters die off all round him.' He is alive, civilised, and very

[20] *Ibid.* p. 116.   [21] *Ibid.*

D. J. Enright: poet of humanism

real, in truth, an extraordinarily normal and healthy man. 'He needs to be if he is to think about himself so minutely, so intensively, so protractedly, without turning into an absolute monster or dissolving into thin air.'[22] 'A genuine *malade imaginaire* is deceiving himself: Zeno is an imaginary *malade imaginaire*.'[23] He may not be much of a tragic figure but his comic potentialities are enormous. He is thoroughly Triestine and bourgeois and, for a hypocrite, a relatively honest man. 'Tottering on the edge of death, as he likes to imagine, he maintains a zest for living, endlessly fascinated by all the sad and lovely contradictions of human life.'[24] *Confessions*, a masterpiece in a period rich in master novels, is a splendid complex of wit, irony, shrewdness, tenderness and dry compassion. It distils, like the poems of Cavafy, a truth that Enright is much taken with; it is stated expressly towards the end of *Confessions*: 'Life is neither good nor bad; it is original.'

Enright's own feeling for literary originality is seen in his very positive response to the poetry of Stevie Smith, Anglican agnostic and metaphysical nanny, whose best work has the surface simplicity and the subtle quality of the finest bone china. Enright's ability not to be impressed by a different, more aggressive kind of originality is evident in his remarks on Nabokov, made on the occasion of a new publication about him: 'Vladimir Nabokov has written quite a lot about Vladimir Nabokov, and now Page Stegner has written about him too.'[25] In any case, how could a writer whose one subject is himself or his memory of himself, stiffened by a truculent self-righteousness, even when it is coated in extraordinarily novel lacquers, be put on the same level as Kafka, Proust or Joyce – in the way that Page Stegner desires? 'To me it seems further evidence that great gifts can be put to small uses, a mountain of words give birth to a mousse.'[26] Enright, indeed, constantly surprises the reader with the unexpected character of his response, by what is, I suppose, its independent, original, first-hand quality. How temperate and perceptive, for example, in spite of his dislike for documented violence, is his judgement of Truman Capote's lacerating *In Cold Blood*, how inward and grasped his understanding of the sensibility of the enigmatic, ferocious Japanese novelist Yukio Mishima. How odd, on the other hand, that with all his revulsion

[22] *Conspiritors and Poets*, p. 172.
[24] *Ibid.* p. 174.   [25] *Man is an Onion*, p. 78.
[23] *Ibid.* p. 173.
[26] *Ibid.* p. 91.

from the floating, untethered symbol, he should give so sympathetic, so creative a treatment to Malcolm Lowry, and such an aptly appreciative one to the rather droning symbols of the Norwegian Knut Hamsun.

It may be that this scope and variety of sympathy is evidence of the activity in Enright's criticism of the connection of life and literature. When there is the presence of one in the other he is capable of detecting it. Certainly a conviction about the connection of literature with life, of the dependence of the originality of one on the uniqueness of the other, is the substance of the standard Enright brings to bear all through his critical work. It accounts for his abhorrence of the purely aesthetic view of literature, especially in its modern form, that the poem is an artifact (what else could it be?), for his dislike of those who attribute importance to technique divorced from material, and for his constantly according to subject-matter and intelligence the importance they deserve. 'Poetry without a subject soon degenerates into verbal onanism.' His high estimation of Wilfred Owen, who certainly had a subject, comes in part from this.

> I heard the sighs of men, that have no skill
> To speak of their distress, no, nor the will!

So also does his discriminating appreciation of Lawrence as a poet. If Lawrence lacks technique in 'Ballad of Another Ophelia', in 'Whether or Not', in 'The Ship of Death', in his marvellous poems on animal modes of life, on mosquitoes, on bats and goats ('Has any other writer gone so far along this road? The insight is uncanny, a sort of magic, like Adam among the animals') then so much the worse for technique. This too is why Enright so much approves of Robert Graves, the outsider, the lone wolf, in whom the relationship of art and life becomes a device for survival.

It isn't those who make the most noise who are nearest to madness. And the neighbourhood of madness, and the sober consciousness of it, is what leads to poetry. Not a preoccupation with some sort of Tradition, not the proud possession of a theory of literature, and certainly not the ambition to cut a figure in the literary-cum-social world. It is, to put it baldly, a late manifestation of the instinct to survive – the poet is the man who has most accurately gauged the odds – and to survive with some honour.[27]

Perhaps like the china plate in Graves's poem, which needs to be

[27] *Conspirators and Poets*, p. 60.

used, to be part of a real existence, and not to be stuck on a shelf in a museum, poetry too needs to soldier on in the effort to win

> a degree of order...of mere comprehensibility, out of the surrounding anarchy; to secure a modicum of temporary mercy from the midst of cruelty, to tame one small beast in a jungle of wild beastliness. 'Poetry... is not the expression of personality,' Eliot wrote in that same essay, 'but an escape from personality.' Perhaps that was an appropriate way of putting it in 1917. Today, one would rather say, perhaps, that poetry is not the expression of personality – who wants to *express* it? – but the preservation of it against those forces which in their different ways, whether savage or kindly, are out to kill it. Poetry is written on a battle-field, not in a library, not in the imaginary museum crammed with all the cultural objects of the past which you must have fingered carefully one by one, the theory has it, if you wish to be more than minor and provincial these days.[28]

The intimacy of literature and life, and therefore the importance of subject-matter, counts both as a positive and negative pointer for Enright. Cyril Connolly, a writer obsessed with 'style', is a skilled phrase-maker lacking in subject-matter. Connolly, whom Enright describes as a very charming and amusing masochist, talking of himself in rather the same way as Auden used to talk about other people, confesses himself to have a passionate belief in art and a contempt for the subjects about which art is made: a contempt, that is, says Enright, 'for life, with its soiled and twitching hands'. If subject-matter or experience or life or something to say is essential for the writer, so is taste, the discriminating response to form *and* matter, essential for the critic. Perhaps one should say not so much taste as propor-tion, an intelligent sense of the proper connection of literature and life, a grasp of the weight to be given to manner and material, and a feeling for the due symmetry between them. About Dylan Thomas, of whom Enright says gravely 'I shall take the liberty of referring to him by his surname', and who is not to be confused with the far more famous phenomenon known as 'Dylan', Enright reports his reaction as the feeling not that the verse is marvellously spontaneous and flowing but rather that it is laboured and unwieldy, so that the way he says a thing is out of all proportion to what he is saying. It is when there is so little argument to get a grip on that commentators most frequently resort to the interpretation of his symbols which – 'such is the nature of symbols, or of commentators' – turn out to be chiefly

[28] *Ibid.* p. 59.

sexual. 'How odd that in this age of precision instruments in literary criticism it is still supposed that to call something a symbol is to make a meaningful statement.'[29] For Enright the right view is Ezra Pound's when he held that the natural object is the adequate symbol. Proportion in the critic, the lack of it in what he is considering, and the friction between the two, lie at the back of Enright's nicely puncturing deflation of the more ballooning kinds of current nonsense and local gods. Lawrence Durrell's *Alexandria Quartet*, for example, less its aesthetic and metaphysical confectionery, would make one novel, just as Henry Miller's *oeuvre*, less the excrement and much of the mysticism, would make *one* book. But the editor of the Durrell–Miller correspondence thinks differently: ' "The complete Durrell–Miller correspondence in half a dozen scholarly annotated volumes will not be ready for publication until the next century . . ." What is going to kill reading in our time is writing.'

If writing is going to kill reading, criticism, at least in some of its later forms, is going to do the same for writing. Criticism since the days of *The Sacred Wood* and *Revaluation* has declined into a frivolous intellectual game. In its complication of technique, withdrawal from a human centre, hypnotised employment of jargon, it resembles nothing so much as some modern philosophical practice, a peculiar exercise, at once hectic and insulated, in which the reader has the impression of witnessing – he can hardly be said to be sharing in – an energetic trance. At the end of this solipsistic agitation he is certainly not much the wiser though he may be less relaxed. An instance of this solitary Greek dancing is quoted by Enright from the journal *Essays in Criticism*, where a critic undertakes to analyse Louis MacNeice's charming little poem 'Snow'. According to the critic it is an intellectual poem presenting a philosophical problem which might require the critic to trace in a treatise the history of the problem of the One and the Many, beginning with Thales. We are told, in the process of the analysis, that in the language of common sense a literal image is a word that stands for a thing: a piece of information which, things being what they are, Enright judges as possibly necessary.

> The room was suddenly rich and the great bay window was
> Spawning snow and pink roses against it. . .

[29] *Ibid.* p. 44.

' "It is only when we come to the word spawning", he [the critic] remarks, "that the trouble begins." If this is what Mr. Cragg [the critic] calls trouble', asks Enright, 'what does he experience when he crosses a busy street? And the trouble is this: "is the image factual, that is, literal, or is it a metaphysical image?" A worker in any other job who asked an equivalent question would be sacked on the spot, without a reference.'[30] This habit of critics to bring bulldozers to bear upon molehills accounts for what Enright calls the suppression of common sense, and indeed the suppression of common humanity as well.

The piece in *Essays in Criticism* is only an ingenuous and innocent example of the grinding of that critical apparatus which can on the one hand prove that the cup of cocoa in *Ulysses* which Bloom offers Stephen is a symbol of the sacrament, or that in the poetry of Shelley it is possible to think of the imagination as being separate from words. Words as mince or poetry without words: what a choice! It seems as if the capacity to walk 'that middle path, where art and nature go miraculously hand in hand' has been almost lost. Perhaps, in Enright's view, we should leave the practice of criticism to the middle men of literature, to the teacher, the journalist, possibly even the reviewer. Certainly at the moment it seems that what we suffer from 'is not a plethora of *Lives of the Poets* but a density of non-Johnsons'. Mass-produced criticism, factitious and niggling discrimination, creates a taste but only for more of the same. It must be added that Enright's possibly undue melancholy about the critical function is accompanied by something like a near-despair about the place of the imaginative writer, too, or at least his sympathetic reference to the views of Norman Podhoretz, editor of *Commentary*, on the future of literature carries such a suggestion: 'The imaginative writer is no longer able to console himself with hopes of posterity, for he feels that the future, if there is one, will be like the present but worse.'[31] He may be read by a few: a few critics.

Enright's concern to re-establish in critical thought the importance of subject-matter in poetry has behind it, or is another way of putting, his sense that the separation of the writer's personal belief from his artistic sensibility, the mind which believes something old from that which creates something new, a distinction insisted on by Eliot some fifty years ago, has

[30] *The Apothecary's Shop*, p. 14.   [31] *Conspirators and Poets*, p. 25.

lasted too long and been taken too seriously. This divorce of belief and art is a newer, sophisticated kind of aestheticism. A writer's beliefs are relevant to what he is saying in a number of ways, some of them by no means obvious. 'Surely, if this were not so, we should be faced with a set of affairs which was simply not human.'[32] What is true of the poet is true of the critic. A literary response is a total response, or as near to it as the critic, the ideal reader, can come. He brings to it all that he is, not only his immediate comprehension and sensibility, but also those crucial sensibilities and regularities which are the grounds of his apprehensions. We cannot be completely free or utterly neutral. Just as our most primitive experience, sensation itself, carries with it the colours of our conceptions and the stain of our past, so our response to a literary work is affected, made easier or more awkward, made possible or even impossible, by the cluster of concepts and assumptions, the 'animating presences' as Henry James called them, which control or influence or qualify our lives. The critic will certainly not be a person unaffected by his own beliefs or immune to those of others. 'On the contrary, let him not refrain from showing his beliefs (as clearly as Leavis shows his moral concerns), without "inhibitions" and without exhibitions. And then, whatever our own beliefs may be, he will have helped us to understand the work he is criticising.'[33]

One belief Enright does not refrain from showing in every aspect of his work, is his belief in liberal, democratic humanism. In him it manifests itself as independence of party and of *parti-pris*, together with that respect for individuality which Coleridge calls 'the religion of the delicate soul'. Among living English poets there is probably no one who expresses this spirit so purely as Enright, among critics none who represents it more wittily and more passionately. Not unexpectedly, a writer with so deep a personal engagement to liberalism must be disturbed by the problem enunciated by the admirable Lionel Trilling: 'For it is in general true that the modern European literature to which we can have an active, reciprocal relationship, which is the right relationship to have, has been written by men who are indifferent to, or even hostile to, the tradition of democratic liberalism as we know it. Yeats and Eliot, Proust and Joyce, Lawrence and Gide – these men do not seem to confirm us in the social and political

[32] *The Apothecary's Shop*, p. 27.   [33] *Ibid.* p. 31.

ideals which we hold.'[34] This is an observation which it is hard to qualify, let alone gainsay, and Enright shows no disposition to quarrel with it. That it is so he takes for granted; that it should be so he acknowledges as part of 'the true mystery which surrounds this matter of a poet's or a novelist's *ideas* as embodied in a poem or a novel and the dubiousness of extracting them and setting them out as plain straightforward statement, political, religious or ethical'.[35] '. . .the poet doesn't affirm, he tells you at the outset that he is writing poetry, not addressing a massed rally at Nuremberg. There *is* style, after all, there is tone, there are conventions. To search through Yeats for fascist tendencies is as rewarding as combing *Tristram Shandy* or *Ulysses* for smut.'[36] These remarks occur in the review of a rather superficial book, *The Reactionaries*, by John R. Harrison, and they illustrate, incidentally, a weakness of Enright's method. So much good criticism appears in the review of books with strictly local or temporary significance that it is very much a case of reading the review, not the book. Imaginative writers illumine patches of experience or of possibility left unreal by political ideologues. In fact one's alarm about the unpopularity of democratic humanism among great modern writers goes with a deepening suspicion that 'a decent, democratic, humanist line, imposed on literature at all effectively, would constitute a formidable tyranny! The dark side of the human soul, working through the imagination, would be wholly off-limits: Lawrence on blood-sacrifice would have to go, and so would a number of our old classics. We should be left to love one another, and die of boredom.'[37] Artists, obsessed with art, living for it as they do, are more conscious than others of difference and inequality, of one poet or painter being better or worse than another. 'The writer is engaged in showing his *difference* from other writers, not his similarity with them.'[38] 'Does literature perform the function of the *memento mori*, is poetry the death's-head of humanism? Will it always be in opposition to any plan intended to better the lot of mankind, whether democratic or totalitarian? If so, then it will serve a useful purpose: even a democracy. . .can cast up scoundrels and seat them in power.'[39]

[34] *The Liberal Imagination*, London 1955, p. 301.
[35] *Man is an Onion*, p. 163.   [36] *Ibid.* pp. 163–4.
[37] *Ibid.* p. 167.   [38] *Ibid.* p. 168.
[39] *Ibid.* pp. 167–8.

When one looks at the variety of books classed as critical, one wonders at the cats' lives (dog's life, too, sometimes) led by criticism; sometimes a submarine creature sunk under the ocean of scholarship; or a gritty tutorial; or a professional contribution to learning; or a lambently enthusiastic lesson. If criticism can be all these, what can it possibly be itself? Nothing, it seems, more than reading, the authentic, articulated act of reading. But readers, according to Coleridge in the beginning of one of his lectures in 1811, may be divided into four classes:

1. Sponges, who absorb all they read, and return it nearly in the same state, only a little dirtied.
2. Sand-glasses, who retain nothing, and are content to get through a book for the sake of getting through the time.
3. Strain-bags, who retain merely the dregs of what they read.
4. Mogul diamonds, equally rare and valuable, who profit by what they read, and enable others to profit by it also.

There is hardly a hint of the sponge, the sand-glass, or the strain-bag in Enright's intelligent and vivacious criticism. It may be he is not always a mogul diamond. Sometimes he may be only an industrial one, cutting a precise and useful line. But on many occasions, on surprisingly many occasions, he is in fact the mogul, profiting by what he has read and enabling others to profit by it also.

4
POETRY II
1960–5

The poems written between 1960 and 1965, collected in *Addictions* (1962) and *The Old Adam* (1965), compose a poetry of pain. If, thinking of its lack of accretion or anything gratuitous, I said of the earlier poetry that it rested on nothing but its own bones, I should have to say about this that it was a bundle of nerves, of nerve-ends, perhaps, sheathed in the lightest cover of silken muscle, and occasionally quite exposed. In some of the poems the formal elements of rhetoric, rhythm, decoration, have been reduced almost to invisibility so that the poems give one the impression of being specimens not so much of Cowper's Divine, as of Clough's Human, and anguished, Chit-chat.

> The stories which my friends compose are very sad.
> They border on the morbid (which, in the literatures
> Of foreign languages, we may licitly enjoy, for they cannot really
> Corrupt, any more than we can be expected to discriminate).
>
> (Sometimes I ask myself: Do I live in foreign countries
> Because they cannot corrupt me, because I cannot be
> Expected to make the unending effort of discrimination?
> The exotic: a rest from meaning.)
>
> ('Reflections on Foreign Literature')[1]

The pared, scraped manner fits a kind of poetry expressive of the human person reduced to a point of suffering or appalled, or sometimes just helplessly irritable, consciousness in the face of the capacity of collective power, State, Committee, organisation, to distribute among ordinary people, impartially, impersonally, often in the pursuit of lofty, abstract ends, injustice, humiliation, and misery. Here are four small clips of verse, three of them which show the horror contemplated and the fourth despair at ever being able to explain the evil.

[1] *Addictions.*

1. Artichokes are being burnt in France,
    to keep the price up.
  As Jews were once incinerated,
    to keep their price up.
  (An average Jew is now worth slightly
    more than before the war.)
                ('Village Classes')

2. In a city of small pleasures,
    small spoils, small powers,
  The wooden shacks are largely burning.
  Bodies of small people lie along the shabby streets,
  An old palace is smouldering.
  Wheeling bicycles piled with small bundles,
  Families stream away, from north to south,
  From south to north.
                ('Brush-fire')

3. To shoot a man against the National Library wall!
  – The East unsheathes its barbarous finger-nail.

  In Europe this was done in railway trucks,
  Cellars underground, and such sequestered nooks.
     ('An Unfortunate Poem (ii) Warm Protest')

4. I – I assure you – speak but as a teacher –
  Lover of learning – in no way any traitor –

  Good God! – don't think that I've an axe to grind –
  It's only – it was simply – merely – never mind.
     ('An Unfortunate Poem (ii) Warm Protest')

The summit of success envisaged in this verse is bare survival, and there is a touch of – something not so strong as hope – perhaps not-despair in the recognition that there is a hard core who do manage to polish this skill.

  You can find them anywhere.
  In better managed states, you'll have to look:
  They're there, unadvertised behind the hoardings,
  In casual self-concealing tenements,
  Asleep by public fountains.
  In badly managed states, they walk the streets
  Free citizens, free to beg.
               ('The hard core')[2]

But as well as the public grief, there is the private hurt: *Addictions* includes a set of eight poems, 'Green Belt', 'Star

[2] *Ibid.*

Chamber', 'A Fine and Private Place', 'A parked car', 'Making love', 'A Chinese Superstition', 'The virtue of a vice', 'One's own people', which ponder, or pick at, a scarred and fruitless love. As my term 'pick at' implies, there is an element of compulsion in these poems and the characteristic buoyancy is diminished. And yet the technique in these is quicker, freer and easier – signs of despair a degree more amenable to art – than in the larger, less graspable issues of public calamity. At the same time there are poems in this collection which appear as tokens of a possible reconciliation between poet and suffering, moments when he succeeds, or nearly succeeds, in achieving within himself a rhythm and balance of a less personal, less harassed kind: a precarious identification with another human being or with a place or situation. One such is 'Dreaming in the Shanghai Restaurant', which testifies to the poet's admiration for an elderly, calm, satisfied Chinese gentleman:

> He wears a gold watch with a gold bracelet,
> But a shirt without sleeves or tie.
> He has good luck moles on his face, but is not
>   disfigured with fortune...
> Some of the party are his children, it seems,
> And some his grandchildren;
> No generation appears to intimidate another.
> He is interested in people, without wanting to
>   convert them or pervert them...
> He walks to the door like a man who doesn't fret
>   about being respected, since he is;
> A daughter or granddaughter opens the door for him,
> And he thanks her.
> It has been a satisfying evening. Tomorrow
> Will be a satisfying morning. In between
>   he will sleep satisfactorily.
> I guess that for him it is peace in his time...

In another the poet stands in the rain-cooled grass under some graceful trees and helped by good music from the gramophone finds out, or almost finds out, what peace is:

> Peace to think in is an awkward gift.
> I wonder: what am I addicted to?
> Fitting others with the things that I don't want,
> Men with peace, trees with adjectives,
> Varying heathens with a varying god?
> The trees dismiss me with a graceful nod.

('Addictions')

Perhaps I have been too positive in calling these last two poems tokens of reconciliation. I am inclined to think on reflection that they are half stops, points of temporary arrest, on the gradient leading the poet to depths where he can contemplate deliberately the act of suicide. In this harsh phase of the poet's art and life, since the sharp distinction made by Eliot between poet and sufferer is less than appropriate in this case, self-destruction seems both natural and sane.

> He walks towards the abyss.
> Because, he's told, he owes it to himself.
> And because he owes it something,
> Because he is drawn by depth and darkness.
>
> ('The Abyss')

But just as intimations of something else assuage or modify the total misery of public and private hurt, so the appeal or the obligation or the single choice of suicide admits possibilities and calls from different worlds with other imperatives. These may be routine duties, or common accidents or a challenge presented to the imagination:

> The abyss will have to wait. Though he hears
> Its voice, like a waterfall heard by a child.
>
> So he retraces that boring stretch of road.
> Something inside him starts to lick its lips.
> He cannot frame an unpainted picture,
> But he frames a rough blurb and a fine critique.
>
> And here at last is the end of the road!
> – It is the end of the month as well,
> There are cheques to be written out.
> Can't they wait? He admits they could.
>
> But a crowd presses at the abyss.
> Dangling their plumb-lines, fishing
> For samples of its sides and bottom.
> No use hanging about. He'll come back later.
>
> ('The Abyss')

Before I leave this subject for good, the poet not just as contemplator and evoker of, but also as participant in, his own end, I ought to refer to another poem, 'Visiting', printed in the second collection of this period, *The Old Adam* (which I shall come to shortly). 'Visiting' is a less harried, better finished poem, in which the experience of the thought of suicide has gone a stage beyond the raw state in which it is present in 'The Abyss', where it gives the impression of having been plucked out before it was ready for treatment, and where it seems less a poetic theme than a diary entry. What is absolutist, compulsive and symptomatic in 'The Abyss' becomes in 'Visiting' relative, mastered, and developed. In particular 'Visiting' is for all its compression more active, at once larger in scope and fuller in differentiation. It seems, too, to obey more nearly the injunction Enright received from his admired Chinese, 'self-pity: the only subject to avoid'.

> Mixing briefly with some
> Who've lived for months, years, ages,
> Deep down in the abyss,
> On lower ledges,
>
> He finds them easy,
> Understanding, even almost gay.
> How can this be?
> He feels the ground slipping away
> From under his feet.
>
> So likeable, so considerate,
> Yes, even almost healthy
> (All their suicides unsuccessful).
> How on earth can this be?
>
> Unless they're visitors from above,
> From the gayer, easier flatland?
> And he the old dweller in abysses
> – Apprehensive, prudent, pained –
> On one of the upper ledges?
>
> Well, that would explain
> The odd resentment they arouse
> In him. And the faint ancient pain
> Of drawing breath. And his ragged nails.

The very free use of quotation I have made in this chapter, which the reader may think my commentary has only abstinently interrupted (or, of course, he may not think that at all), is meant both to illustrate a given point at a particular place and also to offer the reader the chance to recognise the different tone, the greater degree of acerbity, the altogether more thorny manner of this period, odd resentment, ancient pain, drawing breath and ragged nails. The cheerful, stricken occupant of the middle ground, whom I describe as the representative *persona* in

Enright's poetry of an earlier stage, has become more grimly desperate:

> I can see him –
> Drunk and roughed up, because he exercises
> The right to drink, to cut up rough (a little)
> And be roughed up (a lot).
> I see him, and his rigorously dissipated life,
> In a house full of mistresses and cats and dust
> And unpaid bills (a man who liked an orderly life,
> Loved peace, detested debt, was undersexed).
>
> ('The Last Democrat')[3]

The old human habits of *naïveté* and even living now seem in the society observed by this angry eye to be being given up; the poet feels he lives in a world in which the only human habit left will be death. This is the bearing of a beautifully balanced, light but deeply serious poem in *Addictions*, 'I was a gulli-gulli man's chicken'. (And is there any other poet, by the way, for whom the common chicken has been so rich and significant a figure? If Lawrence with his bats and goats and mosquitoes is Adam naming the animals, Enright is the thrifty, patient Eve hand-rearing the hens.)

> Come to terms with one's environment, you say?
> Grass, grit and weather should be my environment:
> I find myself a card, any card, in any pack of cards.
>
> My master cannot do more than he can do.
> (The greatest of beings suffers his own limitations.)
> My master has almost come to terms with his environment...
>
> They have invented toys which look like us.
> It's little wonder that we living creatures
> Should be held as toys. But cheaper, cheaper.
>
> So I have come to terms with my environment.
> Which is: hands that grasp me like a wheel or lever,
> And an early (but at least organic) disappearance.
>
> ('I was a gulli-gulli man's chicken')[4]

It may be that I have concentrated too narrowly on subject-matter in these poems, perhaps in obedience to Enright's critical view which I referred to in the last chapter, perhaps because I

---

[3] *Ibid.*

[4] Gulli-gulli man: travelling Eastern entertainer, snake-charmer and sleight-of-hand man. His speciality is to conjure chickens from the clothes of the audience.

feel that some of these poems are over-personal and sometimes too incoherently involved, like the rather petulant piece which concludes *Addictions*, 'Why isn't your poetry more personal?' Perhaps I should have occupied myself rather more with the poet's intention and procedure: the first which he defines as:

> To bind and probe with rhythms
> What otherwise could not be bound.
> To find and know through images
> What otherwise would not be found.
>
> ('Tout Comprendre')[5]

and the second which is, as he puts it:

> To strike that special tone,
> Wholly truthful, intimate
> And utterly unsparing.
>
> ('Elegy in a Country Suburb')[6]

A prose statement – the entry in Katherine Mansfield's *Journal* comes to mind – may make a more serviceable explanation: 'I want to be nearer – far nearer than that. I want to use all my force, even when I am taking a fine line.' One poem which seems to me to bind and probe with rhythm *and* to strike that special tone, is the short, penultimate one in *Addictions*, 'What might be the first night of autumn'. Here it is:

> As the squirrel can tell that winter nears,
>   and age,
> Trundling some few last ever heavier nuts.
>
> The heavy blind, which holds the night back,
>   holds my gaze.
> Big unlikely painted blooms! Big painted memories!
>
> Does coldness draw you into an ever narrower room,
>   shorter lines and a recurrent rhyme?
> Other tight fixes, of another kind, still lie in store.
>
> So much is free still. Verse, to wit. That element
>   never, for you, stabled in isolation.
> We're compounds. Shoulder to shoulder. Fist to eye.
>
> As the squirrel rubs his head. As I draw back the blind
>   – not easy to tell these seasons apart –
> The painted flowers are gone. Instead, neon and some stars.

[5] *Addictions.*
[6] *The Old Adam.*

Force and a fine line, or rather the force of a fine line, used to get nearer and nearer to a small unsparing truth is, in fact, what we see in this poem. The simplicity of the figuration – the squirrel trundling his heavier nuts, the heavy blind, the big blooms, the painted memories – impresses as something honest and immediate, just as the complication of the syntax in the third and fourth couplets and the quick move from first to second to third person suggest care and scrupulous anxiety to be exact. How the pause after 'nears' and 'age' in 'As the squirrel can tell that winter nears, and age', prepares for, and begins, the slowing down of the rhythm in 'Trundling some few last ever heavier nuts' and how the sound repeated in 'trundling' and 'nuts' and the muted echoing rhyme in 'ever heavier' adds to the sense of a more and more unmanageable burden. The changing, checking rhythm, rapid, pausing, steady, works in the interests of activity and against any drift towards softness and nostalgia. The spare treatment suits, and beautifully realises, the perception of man's contingent, tentative experience, as it does the sense of the compounded, manifold nature of the creature. Age and the question it raises about the tighter scope and more repetitive rituals it compels us to, at once fastens attention on other fixes of a different kind still in store for the poet, and the rest of us, but paradoxically also reveals the area of freedom still open: namely, verse, 'That element never, for you, stabled in isolation', and man himself, 'We're compounds. Shoulder to shoulder. Fist to eye.' The reflection in this poem is energetic, the vitality calm, the whole precisely right.

Many of the poems in the second selection of this period, *The Old Adam*, are in the key of 'What might be the first night of autumn', vulnerable, it may be, but less rancorous and altogether more composed than a quantity of the work in *Addictions*. They speak *from* a kind of qualified tolerance or contingent peace, and they speak *of* misgivings, doubts, the grudging company of the Muse, the suspect nature of the poet's activities, velleities and insecurities, a lost or losing liberalism, the condition of unfreedom:

> The free minds
> Tell us freely about their freedom.
> I myself prefer
> To face the fact of my unfreedom,
> And to speak from that.

> ('Alexandrian')

D. J. Enright: poet of humanism

The occasional indiscipline of *Addictions* has been corrected, but there is nothing frozen or lofty. The poems display as well as an astringent self-mockery, that characteristic liveliness of poetic intelligence which can transform a platitude into a promise, a bromide into a puzzle, even a mystery:

> It's not the easy life you think, this sanity.
> Look –
> The streets fall down, and blame you
> In cracked voices for expatriate indifference.
> The lofty trees
> (Which you are ever ready to praise in prose or verse)
> Look down their noses.
> Is the car stopped? Is it the shadows move?
> For twenty minutes you have been talking humanistically
> To a stone-deaf whore.
> Extending your feet to a baby bootblack
> You perceive your shoes have been abducted.
>
> ('Doctor Doctor')

They offer, too, a skater's gliding grace of figure and turn, that wit of movement which surprises us, as in the lines quoted, in the quick modulation of syntax and the alteration of stance and tone. 'Talking humanistically' is what all these poems do. Talking, as they demonstrate, is less grand but nimbler than conversing, more public than meditating, more private than addressing. The humanism they talk – not about, but – of and with, depends on the recognition, alert and sad, of the facts of human limitation: 'alert' in its quickness and freshness of perception, 'sad' because there is no tinge of the I told you so of the more complacent Original Sinner. The name of Cavafy, that congenial soul, is called in aid.

> Imperfect? Does anything human escape
> That sentence? And after all, we get along.

Enright's is a non-euphoric humanism which has renounced large dreams and capacious claims, which can be indignant though not optimistic, at most flinchingly hopeful, and which acknowledges the complicated ambiguities of existence:

> Nothing human is alien to me.
> Except knives, and maybe the speeches
> Of politicians in flower.
>
> Dampness, of decay and growth,
> Arises all round us,

68

Indigenous mist from earth's two-way flow:
Can you make out which is which?
                              ('Political Meeting')

Three different but surely related anxieties about life and art gravel the writer in this period. One had to do with something happening to the nature of man himself, a second with the condition of the writer's own liberalism, a third with the function of his own poetry. We exist, it seems to him, in a world of unabashed evil and violence which, paradoxically and blindly, supposes itself to live according to some theoretical goodness. 'But now we have fallen on evil times/Ours is the age of goody-goodiness.' Most of us, perhaps the poet himself in some unwilling, guilty way, have become in these circumstances either the social-realist who accommodates himself to the one while vaguely supposing he supports the other, or a Mr Weary, occupying 'A watertight aquarium/Where fish eats fish', who finds that to be a doer is merely to do harm. The seven devils have been cast out from a house swept and garnished by psychiatry and social engineering, every incoherence has been explained by an expert; the one sound disturbing the hospital silence is the 'vituperative humming' of politics. Or as Enright puts it in *Conspirators and Poets*:

...we should remark that a woman who has been sterilized will not produce a baby. An artist who has been successfully psycho-analysed will not produce any more art. A society which has been thoroughly swept and garnished, brought to a high degree of spiritual hygiene, will not produce any art. Remove all the 'dirt' from a human being, and you will be left with an invertebrate.[17]

Man, or the nature of the creature, is being cleared of the old Adam:

They are planning to kill the old Adam,
Perhaps at this moment the blade is entering.

And when the old Adam has ceased to live,
What part of us but suffers a death?

The body still walks and talks,
The mind performs its mental movements.

There is no lack of younger generation
To meet the nation's needs. Skills shall abound.

[17] Pp. 50–1.

69

> They inherit all we have to offer.
> Only the dead Adam is not transmissive.
>
> ('To Old Cavafy, From a New Country')

Times have changed. 'The abstract enmity alone is real/And quite lost sight of, bare forked man.' Dialectic has succeeded dialect. The poet, not a professional or doctrinaire admirer of any heroic past, recalls the helplessness of the serfs subjected to inexplicable tyrannies.

> But times have changed.
> Everything is explained to us
> In expert detail.
> We trail the logic of our lords
> Inch by inch.
>
> The serfs devised religions,
> And sad and helpful songs.
> Sometimes they ran away,
> There was somewhere to run to.
> Times have changed.
>
> ('Change')

In an earlier, effective and affecting poem, in *Addictions*, 'Bright young dull old things', the poet questions the meaning not of the public, chronological past, but his own private one. What was it really like?

> – It wasn't that glass clarity,
> That continence of diaries, those principles
> Subscribed to like the weekend's magazine,
> That conscious charity.

It was something more savage and more withering, making the poet more and more conscious of a kind of constriction, a discolouring of the edges, even some trouble in the centre, of his private liberalism. Those bright, confident certainties begin to look in the face of the movement of this century and its brutishness and stupidity, attenuated and sad. Once he had his finger on the pulse – 'The pulse of a large and noteworthy people':

> That was long ago. Today I'm as you find me.
> All my articulations flapping freely,
> Free from every prejudice, shaking all over.
>
> ('The Ancient Anthropologist')

Not only the shape of a man's conduct but even the patterns of nature seem to raise questions about the propriety or the sense of liberal, gentle humanism.

Humanism has much to recommend it,
But we hardly want it hanging around
In a poem.

('Works Order')

Or, indeed, even hanging around in life. There is an unportentous poem which treats this subject lightly, precisely, drily but in a way which gets from it all the fullness and meaning the subject will bear and the temperament of the poet allow. It begins with a glimpse of the outside, accurate, casual, dreadful; it glances inwardly and deprecatingly at the poet's agitated, liberal sentiment and with an unfussy objectivity, calls the poet 'you', and his habit 'your rule', thereby putting him in his place in the picture; and it finally reflects on the force which drives the creature's nature, which also puts his liberal attitude in *its* place:

Seeing a lizard
Seize in his jaws
A haphazard moth,

With butcher's stance
Bashing its brainpan
Against the wall,

It was ever your rule
To race to the scene,
Usefully or not.

(More often losing
The lizard his meal, not
Saving the moth.)

Now no longer.
Turning away, you say:
'It is the creature's nature,

He needs his rations.'
And in addition
The sight reminds you

Of that dragon
Watching you with jaws open
(Granted, it is his nature,

He needs his rations),
And – the thing that nettles you –
Jeering at your liberal notions.

('A Liberal Lost')

D. J. Enright: poet of humanism

From the nature of man on which poetry has to be based, and
the poet's convictions about it with which the poetry should be
filled, it is a logical step, even for a poet so natural and flowing, so
unselfconsciously spontaneous as Enright, to concern himself,
particularly in our time, with the activity of poetry itself. There
are something like a dozen poems in *Addictions* and *The Old
Adam* which reflect the poet's troubled consciousness on this
matter and his efforts clarify the obscurity it lies in. If we live in a
time of collectives and prose, or of committees and the prosaic, in
a time of crisis requiring that our needs be classified non-
poetically by sociologists and plain men, what is the point of the
poetic? If we have to understand each other massively and coolly,
what are poems for? Hardly to make public alterations in the common landscape. Perhaps to be no more than accessible evidence of
activities as intimate to the individual and engaging much the
same parts of him, as breathing, thinking, feeling. It is true that
'Odd poems still swirl past, / Minority reports, on history's dis-
charge' but it seems more likely that poetry is guessing, trying,
expecting, as suggested in the poem 'Poet Wondering What He is
Up To':[8]

> – A sort of extra hunger,
> Less easy to assuage than some
> – Or else an extra ear
>
> Listening for a telephone,
> Which might or might not ring
> In a distant room
>
> – Or else a fear of ghosts
> And fear lest ghosts might not appear,
> Double superstition, double fear
>
> – To miss and miss and miss,
> And then to have, and still to know
> That you must miss and miss anew
>
> – It almost sounds like love,
> Love in an early stage,
> The thing you're talking of
>
> – (but Beauty – no,
> Problems of Leisure – no,
> Maturity – hardly so)

[8] *The Old Adam.*

72

> – And this? Just metaphors
> Describing metaphors describing – what?
> The eccentric circle of your years.

Not that this personal art of the miniature, of cultivating the windowbox, is either easy or ever very successful. Others may lose their innocence, and gain in skill, 'But not the poet, the battered virgin.'

> Experience makes far-sighted.
> Reality is near, or not at all.
> The air is thick with telescopic visions.
>
> ('A Little Thing')[9]

Infinite difficulty attends the effort to define the tiniest truth, or to grasp it without spoiling it,

> (Truth being what it is,
> Not wholly sweet,
> Not lying quite too deep
> For taint).
>
> ('Silences')[10]

When there is a sparse achievement, it is as much a question of the quality of the silence, of what is unsaid, as of the shape and sound of the utterance. And all that the poet has to help him, Enright suggests, is the feeble strength of a set of weak characters, his own as well as those of the words he uses.

In stressing the lean and harsher line of these poems I shall have given the reader a distorted account, if I have failed, as I think I may, to remind him of that other side of Enright's nature, which neither private pain nor general calamity can quite dismantle, and which shows itself in the snap of wit or in a softer, humorous bloom. Even his irritable poems testify to his being a comic recidivist. There is a considerable clutch of poems, distributed through both these volumes, for example 'Dreaming in the Shanghai Restaurant', 'The Fairies', 'Pitchfork Department', 'Parliament of Cats', 'A piece of advice to aspiring beach-combers', 'Small Hotel', 'The Muse Drops By', which are vivacious and amusing, getting their sharpness from an acute sense of discrepancy between pretension and fact, and their crispness of comedy from displaying engaging patterns made by the freckles of simply being ordinary or the complex stains presented by a muddled humanity – exercises, as it were, in

[9] *Addictions.*　　　[10] *The Old Adam.*

Rorschach laughter. Sometimes, as in 'Dreaming in the Shanghai Restaurant', 'Pitchfork Department', 'The Fairies', the comic tone is the staple of the poem, in others it filters into a very different sort of spirit, as for example the following lines in 'Political Meeting',[11] which set in a disconsolate and sceptical context yet offer a near-Chaucerian blend of kindness and definition:

> Laughter coughs through the mist,
> Students hoot genially, a child falls
> Out of a tree, bulbs and innuendoes crackle,
>
> And solemn pressmen keep the score
> (The workers, perhaps, are working).
> We all behave in the manner expected of us.

On the other hand, ordered to choose a representative poem of this period, I should not go for one in this lighter vein, true as this is to Enright's nature and central to his larger achievement. My choice would be a greyer, edgier poem, in which the public world intrudes, the private world resists, the natural world impersonally continues its ferocious operations, while the subject, on whom these very operations are being performed, keeps the three spheres in intricate and significant play. Here is the poem 'Misgiving at Dusk':[12]

> In the damp unfocused dusk
> Mosquitoes are gathering.
>
> Out of a loudspeaker
> Comes loud political speaking.
> If I could catch the words
> I could not tell the party.
> If I could tell the party
> I would not know the policy.
> If I knew the policy
> I could not see the meaning.
> If I saw the meaning
> I would not guess the outcome.
>
> It is all a vituperative humming.
> Night falls abruptly hereabouts.
> Shaking with lust, the mosquitoes
> Stiffen themselves with bloody possets.
> I have become their stews.

[11] *Ibid.*   [12] *Ibid.*

Mist-encrusted, flowers of jasmine glimmer
On the grass, stars dismissed from office.

The first brief couplet sets the scene and points the mood: a moment, doubtful, hesitant, poised between a vague absence of light and a vague present of dark, the general plangency of which is infringed on by the sting and whine of the insects, and then bruised by the bullying loudspeaker: the loud voice of politics with its large words – party, policy, meaning, outcome – which make for the poet, bitten by misgivings and mosquitoes, a crescendo of incomprehension. In this second section the swing of the phrases, from *If I could catch...* to *I could not tell*; from *If I knew...* to *I could not see*; from *If I saw...* to *I would not guess*, performs the function of a chorus and brings in the movement and the interests of a communal world. In the third section that social noise, in its menace and ugliness, is assimilated to the bloody activity of the mosquitoes, both of them feeding on the poet. This third section is an extraordinary and powerful utterance of the way in which individuality becomes a gobbet to be fed on; implacable politics and remorseless insects must have their blood. 'I have become their stews' is a statement as strong and authentic as Gerard Manley Hopkins's 'my taste was me'. The exquisite close of the poem, in which the vaporous night is given substance and the crispest shape by the flowers of jasmine, and in which the last ironic metaphor – 'stars dismissed from office' – also dismisses politics itself, evokes a kind of peace, out of and in spite of individual suffering and communal busybodiness. The poem moves without jar or oddity from damp dusk and needling insects to mist-encrusted jasmine, from the mechanical booming of politics to stars dismissed from office. It goes, that is, from living, damp, unfocused, stinging, smothered, to a shining strangeness of existence: from the plain to the mysterious. What makes this possible for the poet and acceptable to the reader is on the one side Enright's uncompromised honesty of reaction – he may be fractious or contrary but never devious or tricky – and on the other his courtesy to the reader, a beguiling blend of frankness, self-deprecation and supple expressive skill. There is too his gift of proportion, an instinct for the due weight, the correct pressure, the appropriate response – qualities at the heart of these sane, sad poems.

And so we see, we see we stand as we
have always stood –

D. J. Enright: *poet of humanism*

Paused at Eden's populous gate,
Escorted no inch further, no less far,
Less knowing than we thought we were,
   remembering more;
Seeking as much precision as the subject
   can admit.
And meeting after and before
   – in moonlight's different clarity –
Plain mysteries.

('Bright young dull old things')[13]

[13] *Addictions.*

5
FICTION

D. J. Enright is a writer: not so much of a truism as it might sound when one remembers the names of a large number of other, contemporary novelists to whom writing appears either an unpleasant or untried habit! His primary significance is, naturally, as a poet; he is, in addition, as I have indicated, a fine critic of considerable scope. His talent has also shown itself in fiction, and while one would not want to claim for this a place equal in importance to his poetry and criticism, it is work which displays another side of his distinctive sensibility. His four novels, which appeared between 1955 and 1965, while they have had considerable critical acclaim, have received less than their due attention from the reading public. All these novels are set abroad, in Alexandria, the imaginary island of Velo, or Bangkok or Japan. No doubt this fits in with the simple biographical fact that Enright has spent a considerable part of his career abroad as a Professor of English Literature in various Far Eastern universities. He undoubtedly knows what he is talking about. But it is also in keeping with his reflective, poetically sensitive and coolly registering mind. He is a writer who believes that 'civilization consists in the diminution of human tears', and his response to Far Eastern life contains a quite unsentimental pity for the harsh life of the poor, a cool antagonism for affectation and power whether of academics or politicians, and the small and human virtue of hope, offered by Enright with a characteristic mischief – or flippancy, as some call it.

'The four novels I have published are all really travel books, I am afraid'[1] is Enright's own comment on his fiction. This is an unduly modest dismissal of work in which the execution is finished, the writing light and elegant, the comedy smoothly evolved and the product of an individual point of view, the

[1] *Contemporary Novelists* (ed. James Vinson), London 1972, p. 393.

characters clearly projected, the values humane and coherent, the effect tartly different and original. And yet Enright's deprecating remark makes a point of substance about his first novel, *Academic Year* (1955). It is not so much that it has to do with travel as with a peculiar consequence of a certain kind of travel, that which makes a man an expatriate. Alexandria, the university, the academic year, the people well off or poor, that is, the place and its life, are seen through the eyes of three expatriates, Brett, a cultural officer destined for success though liable to bring disaster to others, Bacon, the long-serving university teacher, 'a rather unofficial kind of man', and another, younger university teacher, the spiritually youthful Packet. On each of the three the city makes its own impression. Brett sees it as *different*, sometimes horribly different, in its cruelty, violence, lawlessness, venality; Packet sees what is unique in it and mostly good; Bacon, the failure, the good man ruined, sees what is common or universal in it. Their separate views, wittily and sensitively articulated, together make a wholeness of vision and construct a place complete and human in its life, suffering and comedy.

The blend of sad and comic is something one is conscious of throughout *Academic Year*, as is the manner which never fudges the former or misses what is productive of the latter. The effect of the delirious Egyptian city on the three principals is seen with a kind of ironic sagacity or sardonic gentleness. The writer's personal tone is unmistakable throughout. It is one which works from the imagination not towards the document, but it never interferes with, its sensibility seems wholly in sympathy with, the accurate, sympathetic, unfussy registration of experience. Here is a passage from the beginning of the novel which is routine and characteristic and corresponds to what in other writers would be cement, glue or continuo.

At the bottom of the street he could see the Mediterranean – or rather a long white balustrade, with someone sleeping untidily on top of it, and then the sea, deep blue breaking into an almost cruel silver. He must pay his respects to this historical accumulation of water. Oh dear, that really was off-putting: he had very nearly tripped over what remained of a beggar's leg which, from the amount of blood on the filthy bandages, appeared to have been recently amputated. Red ink, in all probability, or from a butcher's shop, sheep's blood or something of that sort. Of course the leglessness couldn't have been faked. But they did it on purpose: some little village south of the city, he had heard, specialized in turning out cripples, who then came up to ply their trade, like Irish emigrating to join the American police. The capital outlay was rather heavy – but they were better off than he was, he imagined.

A stranger's first impression of the city is that he is looking at a vast account book: debit and credit side by side, and sizeable sums in each column. For at first there seem to be only two things which, whirling, colliding, shoving one against the other, make up its life. Beggars in various stages of incompleteness, and large American cars fitted with that Middle East speciality, a type of klaxon modelled on the cinema organ. The breeze was growing fainter, Brett felt, the sun less kindly, the silver knives of the sea were glinting more sharply; and the little noises which he had found so jolly when he stepped out of the hotel were now merging into one long continuous roar.

But of course it was only the stranger who noticed the beggars and the automobiles. The inhabitant's more subtilized eye was for different things: Henry Miller set up by drunken Swedes and erratically impressed upon inferior toilet paper, the gentleman driving into the desert with the wife of another gentleman, the latest phase in the war between Coca-Coca and Cola-Cola, the new sambas in the Columbia Music Store (the first word painted out ever since the window was smashed after Colombia's representative at United Nations had voted against an Egyptian motion), the gleaming and often incomprehensible toilet accessories culled from a dozen countries, the level to which the jewellers' shutters were raised – a good barometer of the city's political temperature – or the price of olives. According to one's taste. As for beggars and bashas, they were like the wallpaper in a house. One soon ceased to notice them, and one rarely asked what degree of moral or aesthetic hardening that obliviousness implied.[2]

The urbane air, the lightly bantering tone, the hint of self-ridicule, the continuous moral discrimination, the enticing intimacy of direct address, the flickering wit, the silken run of the voice, the hysterical and absurd details of a city at once brilliant and sordid, the sense of human simplicity and humility in a context of violence, victimisation, extremity – everything helps to manifest the quality of a singularly individual and distinctively moral sensibility. The passage also illustrates how a writer of a very positive personal quality alters the focus of attention, as occasion warrants, and shows the tact with which the transition is managed. At this point Enright is reporting on the arrival in Egypt of Brett, the high-minded, but limited, cultural officer, and his first reaction to Alexandria. The sentence 'he must pay his respects to this historical accumulation of water', in its amused, slightly deflationary touch, is much more Enright than Brett. But immediately after these words the consciousness of the passage

[2] *Academic Year*, pp. 11–12.

becomes more exactly and exclusively Brett's, and turns totally into his at the words 'but they did it on purpose. . .' which precisely define his limited nature and its outraged and abstract liberalism.

Brett is the least sympathetic of the three Englishmen in the novel. He is a neat, upper-class man, theoretically in favour of the poor, of foreigners, of teaching literature abroad, but appalled by what these things turn out to be in practice. He is elastic impossibly pulled in opposite directions. He is one who finds the natural vulgarity of others distasteful and somehow threatening. He blushes in mortification at a luscious performance of 'Irish Eyes' by a Greek singer and an Egyptian orchestra in a popular café, offered in honour of the foreign visitors by players smiling and bowing consciously. (If only it had been 'Greensleeves'!) He wears a pale, thin-lipped, suffering look during a great education event at the Cultural Centre when Bacon, billed to lecture on education, drunkenly recites a very pointed poem, 'Children, Beggars and Schoolteachers'. He feels a mounting sense of the necessity of repudiating this awful man on behalf of himself, the Director, the Centre and England itself. 'But what made such an act imperatively necessary – the presence of foreigners – also made it quite impossible.' It is Brett's screaming nerves, remembering with rage the dirty impudence, the foul inefficiency of rioters and looters, which causes the haphazard death of Bacon at the end of the novel, when Bacon is being vaguely blackmailed by three villagers posing as his mistress's relatives, a situation which Bacon, in fact, is dealing with competently and calmly. And yet Brett does not escape the charity, or better the understanding of the author, whose apprehension of Brett's nature is full and sensitive enough to see in him a certain modesty, earnestness and goodwill. Enright's treatment of Brett, like his treatment of Packet, shows him to have what Henry James called in speaking of Trollope, 'a great taste for the moral question'. Like Trollope he evidently believes that this is the basis of fiction.

Here for example is Packet, the central figure in the novel and the one closest to the author (unless that be true of Sylvie, Packet's girl friend) walking along the Corniche on a late October evening, and showing how the moral, that human instinct to relate anything, everything, to some steadier, larger, finer standard genuinely felt to matter, showing how this instinct, and necessity, wind in and out of every corner of experience, even the minor one of staring at the landscape.

Anything but salty, he reflected, gazing into the sea: no nymphs, no satyrs, no peanut vendors. A pronounced air of retired well-being hung over it: at the same time a light but constant agitation suggested that it could lose its temper at any minute. Honey or wine, Coca-Cola or corrosive acid, but never salty. Never bitter. It was, as the tourist agencies in Europe sang, an eminently pleasurable sea. We have no sympathy but what is propagated by pleasure – the poet's words came into his head – pleasure enlarges the imagination, the imagination is the great instrument of moral good. And no doubt of moral evil. The proposition soothed him. He tried to repeat it, became confused, and looked into the sea instead.[3]

Packet, not unlike the author – although he is not the author – had been born into a vaguely Methodist family, at a time when respectable, fully employed people had still to be called poor. His succession of insufficient scholarships took him to school and university and out of the tight morality of his natural environment into one which, he came to discover, had its own and other proprieties, which themselves required unlearning almost as soon as they were mastered. He felt like a case of retarded development. To which his friend Bacon, an old Egyptian hand of twenty odd years, a patient, humorous teacher, a failed husband, an unpublished scholar, an unsuccessful man, would reply: 'So is everybody else who develops. Don't flatter yourself, Packet.' Packet's development towards his own, lighter, scatter-brained version of Bacon's solid goodness is drawn with a light, confident line against a background of dim, lethargic movement in the University faculty, incessant student strikes, often punctured by strokes of personal goodwill, against the babble of intellectual parties and long, bibulous sessions in restaurants, of terrifying riots set off by something as irrelevant as a Bolivian insult to the Egyptian diplomatic service in the United Nations, of visits to packed police stations or appalling prisons to rescue a student jailed for having a copy of Plato's *Republic*. It is fostered by his relationships with Bacon whom he protects and learns from, with Brett, who offers many occasions for cultivating tolerance and with the girl Sylvie, whom he loves in a friendly, tender, complex way in which sex is a single element and not an abstract dimension.

Indeed, it is the character of life as it is revealed in this novel to flow from one order to another, for it to touch and become

[3] *Ibid.* p. 41.

experience of another kind: evidence this of the concrete, poetic, relating habit of Enright's intelligence as a novelist. At one point Bacon, who is more than most conscious of ours as an age of inhuman abstraction, is reflecting on his years in Egypt. 'Another half-hour passed by while Bacon's thoughts revolved in the same painful circle, all the events of his twenty odd years in Egypt translating themselves into moral comment. . .' Just as events flow into moral comment, so the fluently conversational manner moves naturally from reflection into scene, the freedom of talk, as it does in life, taking drama in its stride. There are some extraordinarily fine and effective scenes, not quite set-pieces and certainly not tableaux but a kind of thickening and thrumming of the narrative line. These may be grim like the riot in the city, with students and bemused peasants fighting soldiers, sticks and stones against tommy-guns, with the poor and dishonest making for the nearest shop windows, to be joined a little later, honesty finally thrown overboard, by the poor and the honest; or they may be deliriously comic like the preparation of the university final examinations in which to avoid the scandalously common circulation of question papers, the process of printing, more exactly, of duplicating, had to be carried on under conditions of extreme secrecy and discomfort in a small badly lighted and unventilated room, amid stocks of paper, stencils, sealing wax, dirty old buckets and metal seals, at the risk of fire, suffocation and the constant breaking of security regulations. These scenes are never simply limited to one mode. The description of the horrors of rioting and looting admits compassion for the mother mourning the shot child she had sent to steal, the account of the gasping absurdity of the university bureaucracy encloses a wry acknowledgement of small officials at any rate doing their bumbling best.

Perhaps what I have been saying is no more than a clumsy application of Eliot's well-known description of wit: 'a realisation, implicit in the expression of every experience, of other kinds of experience which are possible. . .'[4] But if Enright is witty in this way he is also witty in the other, less philosophic way, which enlightens art with amusement, crisp or caustic, or even consolatory: 'Surely something more impressive than crocodiles could be hatched out of that rich mud' reflects the newly arrived Brett as he idles along the side of the sea, thinking vaguely of

[4] 'Andrew Marvell', in *Selected Essays*, London 1934, p. 303.

discussion groups in East London, and poetry readings in the Black Country. Wit and then charity: this is the combination of qualities rare in the contemporary world, which marks Enright's work in the novel. It may be that it relaxes on occasion into witticism and sentiment, though not I think in *Academic Year*, but at its best, at its usual best, it is a most original marriage of intelligence and feeling. It is this complexity too which distinguishes the work from some with which it has been associated. *Academic Year* was called splendidly seedy in the manner of Kingsley Amis when the novel appeared in 1955. But Packet is altogether more complicated, more solidly present than the cartoon Lucky Jim, just as the imagination which fashions him has in it nothing of that negation and cruelty common in the novels of the time.

Generosity of attitude, alertness to discrepancy, the insight of the poet, the knowledge of the inhabitant, the detachment of the expatriate – these things make Enright not only a fine observer of place and society but also a most capable fashioner of character. Character, the steady shape of the person in all his connections and relations, is something Enright's four novels are remarkably rich in, whether it is character which is self-examining and incomplete like Packet's, or formed and densely experienced like Bacon's; or whether it is absurd, gamy and contradictory like the intellectual Marcel, or brisk, efficient, rational and affectionate like the Syrian girl Sylvie in *Academic Year*, or the regal Euphronia in *Heaven Knows Where*. I spoke earlier of being aware in Enright's poetry, for all its spry contemporary spirit, of a traditional wholesomeness of feeling, and of a steadiness of moral centre. In the same traditional way he sees the individuality of the person in the stability of character, his universality in the nature he shares with others. Enright apprehends existence through its consistent shapes and particulars and he works towards a vision of human nature by means of specific forms and humble everyday instances. More modest than those who imitate Lawrence without his genius, Enright is concerned with hewing ordinary practical coal rather than with uncovering the mysterious substance of carbon, or he is concerned with the coal first and the carbon no more than indirectly.

Heaven Knows Where (1957) is Enright's *Utopia*. Packet, jobless after Egypt, answers an advertisement for a teacher of English Literature in the Far Eastern island of Velo. The King of the island is devoted to the *Anatomy of Melancholy* and he accompanies the action with a calculatedly ambiguous and Burtonian commentary upon the life of the community and in particular on the disaster which overtakes his rational and delightful society when it is subject to a managerially modern, political take-over. The inhabitants of Velo represent, or are, the quiet, the amused, the merely human, in contrast to the intellectuals and power maniacs who invade them. The only response the Velonians can make to the overwhelming military power of the Derthans is to fold them into a melting embrace – and it does indeed melt their power away. This pointed parable or analogue of a situation daily to be seen in the newspaper – at least half of it is, the invasion part – confirms in one a sense one has of Enright as a writer with a peculiarly naked sense of actuality. He has the enviably unusual gift of being able to see what is there for his eyes to see. At the same time as he registers the fact he brings to bear upon it a richly orchestrated feeling for human value, at once tender, commonsensical, and ironic.

To be able to see, to evoke, to judge, to be able to let one's fantasy race, though within the limits of a deeper sanity, to have a wild appetite for the ridiculous checked only by an unpatronising generosity – these are certainly gifts helpful to a writer of an unschematic Utopian parable. If we add that the account of the imaginary island is conducted in a prose as well-bred and grave, as supple as Swift's, though without any of the intimations of loathing and disgust which his carries, we can understand how effective and shapely and entertaining *Heaven Knows Where* is. Essentially *Heaven Knows Where* is a defence of the middle position. What it stands for is neither progressive nor reactionary, neither left nor right. If it were to be described in such terms one would have to say that it supported liberality against illiberality, the concrete against the abstract, the individual against the State, the good custom against bad power. The qualities of a good Velonian are specified in the King as 'the absence of self-consciousness...gentle scepticism...chastened modesty...and quiet modest pride'. The people's rituals, festivals and habits are dedicated to the cult of commonsense, modest pleasures, possible improvements. Velo represents a point of equilibrium between defeat and victory, a healthy condition in life.

'True civilization,' I remember the King saying in the course of one of his wilder diatribes, 'is attained when your weapons against disaster are just powerful enough to secure a drawn battle, when defence and attack are perilously and joyously balanced. Defeat means the superstitious and fearful squalor of a savage tribe. Victory is the fearful boredom of a sophisticated society safely pickled in technological brine. Tribes and societies! – that is where melancholy finds its fattest prey, and where the only happy people are those who spend their lives anatomizing it – witch-doctors in the one, priests and prophets and poets in the other...Velo is neither tribe nor society – it's merely persons and things!'[5]

The sunniness and certainties of *Heaven Knows Where* give way in *Insufficient Poppy* (1960) to a bleaker and more troubled obscurity. There is the same fluent and lissom idiom but it draws on harsher sources. It is an effective – much less reflective than *Heaven Knows Where* – an effective, sad novel, closer in mood to Enright's poetry than the lighter *Academic Year* and *Heaven Knows Where*. The sadness which disturbs the even life of three friends in Bangkok, one, the narrator, Roderick, the manager of a family business dribbling away into nothing, who makes a little money by exporting live snakes, another a teacher of English, Harry, who is given the working-class, vaguely nonconformist, Trade Union background attributed to Packet in the first two novels, and another a weird ex-film-cowboy, Colorado Kid, a ruined, inexplicable hulk of a man, is not the small sadness we find every day in every breath, but a large and brutal sadness when one of the friends, Harry, is shot. This calamity shockingly ends the mild pleasures of the trio, conversation, beer, a little opium prudently enjoyed, the odd faithful girl friend, the visits to a provincial city, Thai festivals, all the moderate recreations of the established expatriate in Bangkok. *Insufficient Poppy* is remarkable (as indeed *Academic Year* was in respect of Alexandria) for the tactful indirection with which the life of the place and its people is evoked. There are no set-pieces, no *longueurs*, no explicit descriptions, but we come to have, no doubt because it is refracted through human beings, the clearest vision of the life and the firmest feeling for its people. The novel undoubtedly realises what the narrator, at the beginning of the book, claims is his principal purpose, 'And the chief concern of this narrative is with feeling – the feel of living in a particular place at a particular time.'

The novel has a simple triple structure. The first part establishes the scene, both the immediate pattern of Bangkok life

---

[5] *Heaven Knows Where*, p. 65.

amid the larger context of power and war in the Far East, and the appalling possibilities of holocaust now latent in these things; in the second the action intimates the nature of the moral problem the protagonists are struggling with, which is in essence the unequal conflict of the single soul against the collective and the impersonal. Roderick, the manager of the decaying business, who was shown in the first as relatively detached and uncommitted, is drawn by his friends into an increasingly intimate and searing moral experience. The two friends, the huge, bovine Colorado Kid and the university teacher Harry, are both made mad by the furies. In the Colorado Kid's case his awareness is dim but desperate, and projected in a primitive way on to some, it seems, merely imaginary pursuer, an enigmatically devilish Mr Feilman. Harry, the third member of the trio, feels the moral emptiness of the contemporary world in a highly articulate and finally wholly despairing way. His haphazard death, when he is trying to wrest a revolver away from the possessed Colorado Kid, while it is formally an accident, takes on the air of a deliberate act of sacrifice.

First the scene, then, next the moral event into which it turns and finally the conclusion, rather provokingly called *A Middle*, which is a swirl of memories, opium anecdotes (certainly nothing so grand or decadent as visions), dreams and those small immediate acts of consciousness in which the truth sometimes puzzlingly lies, the agitation of the narrative fitting the now thoroughly engaged, distressed consciousness of the once de-tached Roderick. There is one passage which occurs in a dream in which Roderick is talking with the girl A-Nee, the masseuse in the opium den. They are speaking with that overwhelmingly logical clarity and conviction of the dreamer, in which absurdity and impossibility are quite ironed away, and the peasant girl is utterly at ease making sensitive critical comment on an English poet.

For she was speaking of Edward Thomas, now. (I signalled to a noble waiter: 'Deux Mirabelle...') Of that fine misunderstood man; the quiet, yet so barely contained, misery of his life; of the poems, hardly permitted to come into being, which spoke in such pure accents of overwhelming loss.

She said softly: 'He felt – a little prematurely, perhaps, such a feeling was eccentric in those days – that the world was soon to end. Not merely to change – but to come to an end...'

His was a kind of poetry so difficult to do justice to...(But A-Nee was doing it.) His matter not sorrow so much as the premonitions of sorrow, as sorrow would be felt when it was too late to feel sorrow; all the more desolating because free from personal disappointment or affront; cosmic because growing out of the earth, from the roots of grass, cavities inside hedgerows, old nests, small realities (as small as we). She murmured:

> '*And most I like the winter nests deep-hid*
> *That leaves and berries fell into:*
> *Once a dormouse dined there on hazel-nuts,*
> *And grass and goose-grass seeds found soil and grew.*'[6]

Insufficient Poppy is a disturbing, painful book, at moments even, in the second and third parts, throbbing with intense personal anguish. But a certain blurring of the design and too explicit declaration of bitterness make it a less achieved and more fragmentary success than *Figures of Speech* (1965), which with *Academic Year* is, in my view, his best novel. *Figures of Speech* is decidedly more active as a story, the characters are more engaging, the fiction altogether more embodied and appealing. There are only three characters, in effect, another English university teacher, George Lester, Chung Lu, a high-minded young Chinese scholar, and Mattie, a crisp girl on vacation from Singapore, who displays both the elegance and the forcefulness characteristic of the educated young Chinese woman. The love affair of the two Chinese and the gorgeously comic adventures of George are plaited together with nimble and natural smoothness. There is also an abrasive treatment of George's relations with, and betrayal by, the British Council and the Embassy. The conduct of both towards their own nationals, especially when these are writers, poets and similar dandruffed types, shows unbridled cautiousness competing with unabashed stupidity and composes a not very admirable if highly comic model of British diplomatic and cultural *moeurs*. In addition there is a characteristically sharp and perceptive account of the Japanese mode of entertaining foreigners, which is a marvellous piece of dancing humour and social analysis. It is hard to define the effect of this remarkable book in which an unaffected fastidiousness of spirit is accompanied by the most open and inclusive generosity of response, and in which both are conveyed in an idiom utterly personal and devastatingly witty.

It is the union of flippant and forgiving, wit and pity, in Enright's fiction which gives it its intensely personal flavour of

[6] *Insufficient Poppy*, pp. 178–9.

blended tartness and kindness, or, given the Eastern provenance of so much of it, of its sweetness and sourness. We find this double savour throughout the narrative, in the tone, in the imagery, in the reflections which jink suddenly from melancholy to mordant, in the comic pathos of the account of the closing down of the opium dens, in the bowel-melting funny scenes like George's lecture at the British Council, George being sober and the audience drunk, or in the grimly satirical episode in which the imprudent and, on this occasion, innocent George is beaten up by drunken policemen outside a brothel. (As the last remark suggests, the material of the fiction, like that of the poems, is often related to events in Enright's own life, but they are, in this novel, very skilfully distanced and controlled.) And of course we sense this sweetness and sourness most in the characters: in George, 'a man of feeling but careless of repute', a more sophisticated, slightly hard-bitten version of Packet in *Academic Year* and *Heaven Knows Where*; in the laundry-fresh, incisive Mattie; and in Chung Lu, whose temperament as a young man corresponds to his life as a boy, 'immaculate in behaviour, painstaking, quick, and remote to the point of mysteriousness'. George's humiliation and disgrace, and the creepy disloyalty of his official compatriots, are described with bite but also with glints of gaiety; Chung Lu's transformation as a result of his travels and of his feeling for the attractive and rational Mattie, from his cool state of Chinese superiority and his scholarly dedication to verse, calligraphy and correctness in thought and behaviour, into that of agitated and nervous lover, is shown with a balanced, unpatronising sympathy and a clear eye for every absurdity. Chung Lu is perhaps the most complete and satisfying, as he is the most graceful, character in Enright's fiction. Authentic and ancient in tradition, fine in quality, magnificently Chinese, he is also seen as instinct with a common and instant humanity.

It is now some eight years since Enright published a novel. One must hope that at least a portion of his remarkable creative talent will be engaged in this kind of work again. Perhaps a particular reason for this desire is that Enright's novels are, in a very special way, *intelligent*. By intelligence I mean that liveliness of faculty which combines a measure of wisdom with a sense for the concrete occasion and an intuition which effortlessly brings a cogently human standard to bear on the grasped situation, and it hardly seems necessary to stress why this capacity daily appears more rare and more desirable. This intelligence speaks in all the material of his fiction, just as it does in the actual writing, which joins a lithe, light-footed strength to sensitivity, and sardonic mockery to affectionate recognition. His account of the expatriate life of teachers, their friends, lovers and superiors in Bangkok, Singapore, Japan, is poetically evocative of the places, shrewd in its analysis of them, and at the same time quick with the sense of calamities, public and private, either waiting to trip us up or thronging to mob us. Enright is full of pity for others but wary about self-pity for himself. And he is always aware of the sanitary necessity of laughter. So often in official bad books himself, he feels for the victims of power, and who of us isn't one of those sometime? If intelligence is the principal character of – perhaps the principal character *in* – Enright's novels, the quality most marked in their method and presentation, their effect is to cherish and to foster in circumstances of brutal antagonism the remnants of humanity. Like his intelligence this is something which makes Enright a member of the school of Goethe. There is a passage in *Academic Year* which could well act as an epigraph not only to this chapter on his fiction but to this study as a whole:

That salt destroying sea beneath which nothing could grow, the sea which was eating away at our human coasts, all over the world. By association he thought of the great European reclaimer, that coastguard of humanity who, for once, had united energy with intelligence and intelligence with good will: and Goethe's words came into his head. 'How could man live at all if he did not give absolution every night to himself and all his brothers?'

6

POETRY III
1965–73

The poems written between 1965 and 1971 and published in *Unlawful Assembly* (1968) and *Daughters of Earth* (1972) signal no radically new direction in Enright's mature manner, whether in idiom, method or target, but they do manifest, if not a new, an increased or developed authority and power. Weight in the line, the pressure of a nearly insupportable experience, a poetic rhythm sometimes at the farthest remove from song – these are the qualities of the poetry which speak of an effort to be bare, hard, essential. Even the wit is undecorative and austere.

> The sour breath of the underfed
> Stood in the overloaded roads.
> The farmers sold their daughters,
> Daughters sold their flesh and blood.
>
> In that country one almost came
> To emulate the accents of Brecht.
> Plain speaking was in order,
> Plain speaking was merely truth.
>
> These days things are looking up,
> One sees more cars on better streets,
> Although no revolution intervenes,
> No heroes. Nothing much to write about.
>
> Simply: 'One another we must love or
> Show no profits,' they explained.
> If this put paid to the accents of Brecht,
> Who am I then to complain?
>
> ('The Accents of Brecht')[1]

The heavy, repressed rhythms and the stony laboured phrasing of the first stanza fit the plain horror the poem starts from, the crimes forced upon men by their impudent itch to survive; and

[1] *Unlawful Assembly.*

the unexciting idiom and the flat surface of the rest of the poem are appropriate to the recognition of wrong transformed into something kinder if more commercial. If this transformation is accompanied by the cancellation of heroic speech and if it puts paid to the accents of Brecht, if life *will* make itself awkward as a subject for art, what right has the poet to complain? The last lines are one low-toned version of a theme working in several of Enright's poems (I noted an example in *Some Men are Brothers* in Chapter 2), a misgiving or bad conscience about the facility with which poetry can intrude on human suffering. The capacity of the poet to use other people's suffering as nutriment for his art makes Enright uneasy and even ashamed. On the other hand, he is guiltily aware of the poet's suave gift for gliding around trouble. The indirections of poetry can make the artist miss large sorrows staring him in the face.

> Poets are not concerned
> With the streaks on the tulip,
> The small red appearances.
>
> And the art of poetry is
> Not to say everything.
> Much virtue in obliquity!
>
> If you know already, you can tell
> From this massive obliquity
> That one lives in a time of war.
>
> ('It's an Art')[2]

It is, I believe, uneasiness as to some of the things poetry can do, together with misgiving at how skilfully it avoids doing other things, which, with a temperament incessantly struck by the absurd in life (though never by life as an absurdity), makes Enright, a poet who takes poetry very seriously, that is morally, even in a period as harsh and harassed as this, so quick and so good as a comic poet. Even in this severe volume, *Unlawful Assembly*, he swerves suddenly into the dry banter of 'Processional' or the gurgling bawdy of 'The Mysterious Incident at the Admiral's Party'. Enright is so rich a comic because the wit or the clowning takes place in a context of anxiety and distress, while the graver poems never wholly exclude some engaging absurdity, quite often at the expense of the poet himself. The ingathering,

---

[2] *Ibid.*

connecting quality of Enright's sensibility, shading one set of feelings into another, softening the edges between kinds of things, depends upon a view of life as intrinsically productive of variety and insusceptible to categorisation. Just as experience is incapable of being parcelled out into lots belonging to x rather than y, so words, the poet's material itself, Enright sees as not exclusively the poet's own, a fact he teases at in a poem suggested by the style of working of the great Singapore painter, Cheong Soo Pieng, which contrasts the painter's and the poet's task.

> The Master, within a week,
> Knocks off three paintings,
> Well up to standard.
>
> In his tiny studio,
> Petrol and pandemonium outside,
> And a minimum of view,
>
> Irrespective of situations,
> National pride and income,
> This bloc and that.
>
> How different from us!
> Our stuff the stuff of politicians,
> The cries of maddened cabbies
>
> And spavined academics.
> The whole day goes on washing words,
> Scraping and scrubbing.
>
> ('Rueful Writers Contemplate a Painter')[3]

Washing, scraping and scrubbing, the necessary operations of rinsing and freshening words, are activities Enright, a more than competent housekeeper of the language, is skilled and conscientious in. But whether it is recovering something from the waste or discovering something useful and unused in the language, the purpose of such work is always to preserve some gleam or tremble of life, supremely of human life but not exclusively so: the life of animals and plants comes in for this service too. Here are two poems, 'A Dry Palm', the delicate pressing of a mere whisper of experience, and 'Watcher in the Sky', which uses a favourite technique of slipping, barely-modified repetition and gives an extraordinary effect of spontaneity, gratitude and joy.

[3] *Ibid.*

Fronds are dancing in the wind,
A drawn-out din of movement.
Yet only one of them is heard –

A dead one, all but dead,
Alive by the skin of its sallow foot,
Its carking, carping voice.

A wary veteran, hardly daring
To stir, far less to dance.
But doing all the talking.

('A Dry Palm')[4]

They dart or lurch, collide or embrace
(Beaks long, for what? Eyes red, with what?)
They chirp, they screech, they whistle.

Whether the starlings are
Making love or making war
– That I cannot tell.

They meet or they part,
They give or they take,
They jostle or nestle.

I cannot be sure
– So many of them, so many! –
I know what I like to think.

They are full of life
(One's eyes blur with grateful water)
They are living, lively, full of life.

Off duty too,
Ten twilight minutes for indulgence,
Hand cupped beneath the chin,

Some grander watcher,
Watching us (with maybe grateful, maybe blurring eyes),
Will he know what he likes to think?

They are full of life
– So many of them, so many! –
They are so lively, living, full of life.

('Watcher in the Sky')[5]

In these poems we observe the poet as celebrant of the lively,
the living, the fullness of life, extending a near-Buddhist courtesy

[4] *Ibid.*   [5] *Ibid.*

to trees and birds, as he does elsewhere to cats, dogs, crickets, mosquitoes, lizards, and grateful in a dry and withering world for the mystery they exemplify and declare. The office of cele- bration, however, is but intermittently allowed to the stricken, too-conscious modern poet:

> One works because
> Of lack of leisure;
> Out of loss
>
> Of liberty;
> To fill deficiency
> With presentness.
>
> You need defeat's sour
> Fuel for poetry.
> Its motive power
> Is powerlessness.
>
> ('Cultural Freedom')[6]

Even if poets, as Enright grimly notes in his middle years, have been written off by evolution, even if they are 'sad / And diffident monsters, / Stuck in primeval tear-stirred mud',[7] there are still elements in the sensibility of any considerable poet which are a projection of the psyche of a given period, and which represent faithfully the form pressed upon human nature at a particular time by a peculiar predicament. The figure of the poet as victim which we see in several of these poems, at once sadder and more impotent than the *persona* of the earlier work, is all too appropriate an image for him now. The phrase I quoted above about defeat as the 'sour fuel for poetry' suggests at any rate the special kind of victim this poet is, neither suavely resigned nor gracefully stoic, but jerking with irritability, going down pro- testing, and at the very least recording his desperation. In another solid, intensely feeling poem, 'Back',[8] we have Enright's accurate report of one in this position.

> Where is that sought-for place
> Which grants a brief release
> From locked impossibilities?
> Impossible to say,
> No signposts point the way.
>
> Its very terrain vague
> (What mountainside? What lake?)

[6] *Ibid.*   [7] 'They Who Take the Word', *ibid.*   [8] *Ibid.*

It gives the senses nothing,
Nothing to carry back,
No souvenir, no photograph.

Towards its borders no train shrieks
(What meadowland? What creeks?)
And no plane howls towards its heart.
It is yourself you hear
(What parks? What gentle deer?).

Only desperation finds it,
Too desperate to blaze a trail.
It only lives by knowing lack.
The single sign that you were there
Is, you are back.

The several, sighing questions in the second and third stanzas
make an extra graceful loop in Enright's rapid, flexible, inventive
line; and the plangency they release is markedly at odds with
the direct, driving energy of the main statement of the poem.
The result gives a peculiar effect of complication, 'of locked
impossibilities', and desperate contradiction.

Whether it is the poet in despair or the poet as victim, as
frantic or mocking, as written off or sent up or put down, one
thing is very clear from the poetry, the deep accord which the
poet finds, sometimes to his astonishment, between himself as poet
and man as man, for example in 'Public Bar' in the collection
Daughters of Earth (1972):

Why are the faces here so lined?
Have they ever borne the pains of
Poetry? Or the strains of music.
Their hollow eyes have never searched a
Sombre canvas.

Their souls not scorched like ours
By burning issues. Or their cheeks
Trenched by the tears of things. No
Complex loves or losses wrung their hearts
Like ours.

Why do their faces look like this,
Carved through centuries, whole histories
Etched in their skin? Like works of art
Themselves. How did they steal
Our faces?

Daughters of Earth includes some of the finest of Enright's mature poetry. The poems fall into three groups, Asian poems treating of oppression, war, poverty, and, as one would expect, a set of sardonic and comic poems, and a handful of strong, tragic and intensely personal utterances of private experience. What they have in common is twofold. For one thing they share an extreme precision so that the contour of each phrase, the centre of each image, the slightest rise or fall of rhythm, is defined with an unqualified accuracy. At the same time the line has all of Enright's characteristic mobility and vitality, moving with spontaneous, inward energy and with a variety which never flags. One is reminded in fact of Blake's electric statement, 'the great and golden rule of art, as well as of life, is this: That the more distinct, sharp, and wiry the bounding line, the more perfect the work of art; and the less keen and sharp, the greater is the evidence of weak imitation, plagiarism, and bungling...The want of this determinate and bounding form evidences the want of idea in the artist's mind.'[9] On the evidence of *Daughters of Earth* there is no want of idea in the artist's mind nor any failure of its projection into a wiry and bounding line. Indeed if we put together this linear precision and this bounding rhythm, and join to it an attitude, the deep impulses of which are always on the side of liberality and generosity, so that even in the sharpest, most acid irony there is nothing pinched, mean or sour, we shall have the notes making up Enright's personal tone – 'the accents of Enright', as it were.

I want in a moment to look more closely at an example of each of these three classes of poems from *Daughters of Earth*. But before I do, perhaps I could fill out a trifle what I mean by Enright's personal tone, and add a grace note or two to 'the accents of Enright'. A lapsed Wesleyan and a lurching humanist, as he calls himself, he is also in one part of his sensibility distinctly oriental, an admirer and almost a possessor of a Chinese habit of mind, courtly, exact and ironic. But he is also one formed by a working-class childhood and memories of margarine and hissing gas mantles, an enemy of executives and industrialists, managers, chairmen and senior civil servants. He is without even the thinnest carapace of indifference and almost shockingly vulnerable in his sympathies for the cruelly treated. He is erudite and colloquial, a common man with an aristocratic disdain for moral

[9] *The Complete Writings of William Blake*, ed. Geoffrey Keynes, London 1968 (fourth printing), p. 585.

seediness. He can be the literary equivalent of a comedian in a
working men's club, crackling and vulgar, abhorring the smooth
efficiency of the administrative world *and* a poet whose work is
orchestrated by fitting, quiet allusion to several literatures and
cultures. He is unable to look on wounds calmly or to separate
himself from the suffering of others. He is troubled by the ease
with which print can rant 'late and safely distant' from the
bloody action. 'Bright imitations cram our watering eyes.' His
most precious possession is his share in our common human
nature. He is the fan of soldier ants, red-eyed starlings, calling
frogs, lizards, hawks, bats, and even the intoxicated mosquitoes,
and if he is a servant of any god, it is of Hanuman, the monkey
god. The closest kin I can find for this player of the noodle-
vendor's flute is one who would blend the temperaments and
skills of Burns and Cavafy, a poet of clarity and light, kindness
and angry wit.

Here then, since it is not too long to quote in full, is the first of
the poems from *Daughters of Earth* I have to comment on,
'Children Killed in War'.

> A still day here,
> Trees standing like a lantern show,
> Cicadas, those sparse eaters, at their song,
> The eye of silence, lost in soundlessness.
>
> And then, no warning given,
> Or if foreseen, then not to be escaped,
> A well-aimed wind explodes,
> And limbs of trees, which cannot run away,
> May only hide behind each other.
>
> Grant their death came promptly there,
> Who died too soon,
> That pain of parting was not long,
> Roots ready to let fall their leaves.
>
> The wind burns out,
> The trees, what's left, resume their stand,
> The singers stilled, an iron comb
> Wrenched roughly through their lives.
>
> While you, your thinking blown off course,
> Design some simple windless heaven
> Of special treats and toys,
> Like picnic snapshots,
> Like a magic-lantern show.

The poem begins with a state of tranced stillness, a condition to which the 'lantern show' and the hinted literary reference add the sense of something painted, serene and innocent. The second stanza offers a double contrast, a mild, preparatory one, in the balancing, discriminating qualification, 'and then. . .or if'; and next a totally devastating one in the interruption of the well-aimed wind exploding. The phrase 'a well-aimed wind' combines the suggestion of calculated evil with that of an impersonal act of nature; while the 'limbs of trees, which cannot run away', makes the trees the only too appropriate surrogates for the children. Obliqueness and control make the effect all the more direct and devastating. The third stanza takes up the reasoning, balancing mode of discourse and the quiet, concessionary 'Grant their death came promptly' and 'That pain of parting was not long' offer the calm of a mind just held in desperate balance. The intervening action has changed the dimensions of existence: 'A still day here' has become 'their death came promptly there'. The last two stanzas present what the tranquil paradisial beginning has become, when the iron comb of action has been wrenched roughly through it: that is, both the objective consequence of the bomb, and also, at the end, the subjective consolation of some imagined, windless heaven – a fantasy of despair bitterly projected in the snapshots and the magic-lantern show.

It may be that some of Enright's verse is over-fluent, even chatty, seeming to achieve utterance one moment before an absolute, final form has evolved, but 'Children Killed in War' gets its intensity from its curbed compression. There is nothing over-developed or talked-out in it. And if some of Enright's verse is too flowing, too 'natural', this poem on the other hand is meticulously organised with a severe internal logic, in which each phrase, image, and rhythm draws on and sustains its neighbour and contributes to the total meaning. It may be, too, that Enright seems sometimes a trifle fractious or cross, ingenious in discovering a wrong[10] – one should after all allow the other side the bumbling and stupid humanity one forgives in oneself – but in this poem, where the calamity is beyond the range of indignation,

---

[10] Cf. what Enright himself said about Lawrence: 'It is as if Lawrence sometimes woke up in the morning with a strong and perhaps not groundless distaste for the human race and thereupon wrote out of his irritation not one poem against it but four or five.' (*Conspirators and Poets*, p. 101.)

the protest is all the more moving and powerful for its discipline and silence. I regard 'Children Killed in War' as one of the most richly finished of Enright's poems, and I put it with 'The Noodle-Vendor's Flute', 'Misgiving at Dusk', 'Poet wondering what he is up to', 'First Death', 'I was a gulli-gulli man's chicken', 'Visiting', 'Kyoto in Autumn', 'Desert Cure', at the height of Enright's achievement.

The next poem from *Daughters of Earth* I want to glance at, 'More Memories of Underdevelopment', is a light and occasional piece, but perfect of its comic kind, its difference from 'Children Killed in War' a measure of the poet's scope. All that it has in common with that poem, in fact, is that it springs, like many of Enright's poems, from an event in his own experience. The author is rashly expounding the poetry of Gerard Manley Hopkins to a class of young Chinese Catholics. In 'Children Killed in War' the tragedy required a Job-like patience of attitude and a submergence of the writer's personality. Here, where the writer himself, or the figure he cuts, is one of the two poles of the piece, stoicism becomes tetchy concern and querulous affection for the unwarranted but charming complacency of the Chinese papists. The poem begins by quoting Hopkins's great statement 'God's most deep decree / Bitter would have me taste: my taste was me' and goes on:

> A lapsed Wesleyan, one who dropped out
> Halfway through the Wolf Cubs, and later ran howling
> From Lourdes by the first bus back, whose idea of
> High wit is 'God si Love', who would promptly
> Ascribe the sight of Proteus rising from the sea
> To spray in the eyes or alcohol in the brain –
> Yet these words appal me with recognition,
> They grow continuously in terror.

How much more, then, the poet expects these lines must mean to those born and bred in the faith.

> But no,
> They seem to find it a pleasing proposition,
> The girls are thinking how nice they taste, like moon-cake
> Or crystallised pears from Peking,
> The boys are thinking how good they taste, like crispy noodles
> Or bird's-nest soup.

How ridiculous grumbles the poet that he, the 'lurching humanist', should have to instruct these unworried Chinese

Christians in the doctrine of the fall; how hard that he of all
people is expected to inculcate a sense of sin in those who should
have been nursed on the idea! And what a bloom of appreciative
kindness these lines, for all their narkiness, show: as attractive
and mellow as the taste and look of the fruits the young see themselves as:

> Their prudent noses wrinkle almost imperceptibly.
> Oh yes, they tell themselves, the poor old man,
> His taste is certainly him...
> And they turn to their nicer thoughts,
> Of salted mangoes, pickled plums, and bamboo shoots,
> And scarlet chillies, and rice as white as snow.

This is but one of several comic modes to be seen in all phases
of Enright's work, even the most sombre, his being a temperament in which extremes of flippancy lie beside a shuddering sense
of suffering. Perhaps the wildness of one is connected with the
intensity of the other. In *Daughters of Earth* there is not only the
kindly character-comedy of 'More Memories of Underdevelopment' but also rueful professional memories, both salty and self-
deprecating: of the academic in 'Board of Selection' and of the
professional writer in 'Royalties' and 'Memoirs of a Book
Reviewer'; and in addition the zany linguistic capering of 'An
Ew Erra':

> The trypewiter is cretin
> A revultion in peotry
> " " All nem r = " "
> O how they £ away
> @ UNDERWORDS and ALLIWETTIS
> Without a .
>
> FACIT cry I!!!

The shudder of suffering goes not only with the capacity to
giggle but, more strangely, with an oddly discursive, reasoning
habit of mind. Enright will pounce on a remark or a saying, even
a platitude, and turn it this way and that with a curiosity alert to
the merest quaver of interest or contrariety. He then draws out
one meaning which would certainly have escaped the ordinary
man and lucidly develops it with distinctive but irrefragable logic.
The single, clear line of the argument is partly attributable to his
success in excluding inappropriate significances and partly to his
ability to make each point generate the next. He excavates what

is latent in a meaning in the way some poets extricate what is
implicit in an image. A fine example of this method is a poem
which I believe belongs with his best work called 'How Many
Devils Can Dance on the Point. . .' in *Daughters of Earth*. The
poem is too long to give in full at this point, but perhaps I may
quote the first section:

> Why, this is hell,
> And we are in it.
> It began with mysterious punishments
> And the punishments led to the crimes
> Which are currently being punished.
> The more rational you are
> (What you have paid for
> You will expect to obtain
> Without further payment)
> The less your chances of remission.
> Only the insane and saintly
> Who kiss the rod so hard they break it
> Escape to a palliated hell.
> For the rest, why, this is it,
> And we are in it.

'Why, this is hell. . .': from this unpromising colloquial flatness
Enright develops bleak horrors and icy intensities. The poem has
something of the air of a medieval disputation. A point is taken
up, distinguished, dismissed, or at least part of it is dismissed
while another leads on to a further terror. In fact, as my use of
the term 'disputation' suggests, the poem is an extended, creative
commentary on those four dull words with which it begins, 'Why,
this is hell'. The 'Why' leads to the interrogation which makes
the logical structure of the poem; the 'this' concentrates the
negation of hell into this needle-pointed instant; the 'is' contains
within it the absolute and hopeless state; the 'hell' is what it is.
The phrase 'Why, this is hell' appears again and again to show
that the effort of reason cannot placate or qualify it. Even the
comfort of comparison, the more or less, appears as a final chill
illusion:

> If the other was hell
> Then what is this? –
> There are gradations of Hades
> Like the Civil Service,
> Whereby the first is paradise
> Compared with the last;
> And heaven is where we are

> When we think of where we might have been.
> (Except that when we think,
> We are in hell.)

Neither analysis nor imagination can tell us what function the hideous instant is seen by God or life or what, performing, or why it is required, unless it be to please 'Someone who derives such pleasure / From being thus gratified', so that the explanation may be just the ancient and enigmatic one of God or life or what moving in its mysterious way. Except, the poem coldly concludes:

> Except that –
> Lucid, strict and certain,
> Shining, wet and hard,
> No mystery at all.
> Why, this is hell.

In this poem, in its highly personal speech and rhythm, in its arctic severity of feeling, we hear the authentic clack of the terrible shears. This instrument, however, has nothing to do, or nothing directly to do, with the one spoken of in the title of a set of poems about his own childhood and adolescence which Enright published in 1973.[11] The terrible shears referred to here are not those wielded by the sinister sisters but the tool of granpa's trade:

> When Granpa wasn't pushing old ladies
> Through the streets of the Spa
> He would cut the grass on selected graves.
> Sometimes we went with him. Dogs
> Had done their business on the hummocks.
> The water smelt bad in the rusty vases.
> The terrible shears went clack clack.
>
> ('Uncertainties')[12]

It is right that I should end with these autobiographical poems, that this study should finish where it began, with Enright's life, Enright being a poet who believes that art must be sustained by life and whose own poetry is packed with bits of biography. Of the poems in *The Terrible Shears* perhaps I can say that they are Japanese in form – though closer to the crackling *senryū* than the precious *haiku* – and Chinese in spirit: Japanese, that is, in being brief, spare, and if not exactly anonymous since impressed indelibly with a unique tone, at least unfussed about individuality; and Chinese in feeling, that is, coherent, solid,

[11] *The Terrible Shears*, London 1973.   [12] *Ibid.*

pragmatic, affectionate, objective. I hope the oriental references appropriate to Enright, *savant* and sinophile, will not disguise the essentially English quality of verse set in the glum Midlands in the depressed 1920s and 1930s in a *milieu* where poverty was not only a chronic condition but an unquestioned assumption. In fact the poems, a rare version of common life, appear as a species of poetic sociology conveying the special, pinched and docile quality of one kind of working-class life at the time. Not many red banners here and very little of the bosomy warmth other writers remember from a comparable experience, 'Our folk didn't have much / In the way of lore.' Instead we have an intent and scrupulous respectability, suspicion of oddity, discomfort in the presence of the foreign, together with uncertainty, vulnerability, a state of almost complete exposure to disaster, illness, the loss of a job, an accident at work, a parent's death. Life showed itself as a genteel minefield. Patience was a potent word as well as a favourite game and, it seemed, a cardinal virtue. '*Putting up with* things / Was a speciality of the age.' 'They' were different, powerful, more to be avoided than envied, 'a funny lot, but clever with it'. 'Keep out of THEIR way, child! / Nothing but shame and sorrow follow.' Strong magic attached to the canal and the workhouse, which were real, not literary places.

> How many remember that nightmare word
> The Workhouse? It was like a black canal
> Running through our lives.
> ('Shades of the Prison House')[13]

Class was not so much a concept as an instinct, and as instinct it seemed as much, perhaps even more, an individual than a social one. Neighbours were remote but inquisitive:

> A twitching of meat-safe curtains –
> Whole streets alive with tiny movements.
> ('Curtains')[14]

The fine matrons in the Cadena on Victoria Parade frightened one – and apparently still can according to 'Ancient Fears'. Schoolmasters even when kind appeared to be helplessly patronising to scholarship boys, who found even the ecstasy of childhood in the Infant School blended with humiliation:

[13] *Ibid.*   [14] *Ibid.*

Bowing our heads to a hurried nurse, and
Hearing the nits rattle down on the paper.
('Two Bad Things in Infant School')[15]

Dancing Sellinger's Round, and dancing and
Dancing it, and getting it perfect forever.
('And Two Good Things')[16]

Within this context of desperation there was a family life
sharp in character and tang: granpa who sturdily wheeled the
decrepit round Leamington in a bath chair, and granma who
played crib for hours with the author. She was sympathetic and
doddering and had to be removed to the workhouse by force but
was found to be deranged on arrival so that she did not land
up there after all: this was an escape from the ultimate shame.
There were also country cousins – it was still possible in such a
place to have a real connection with the rural world – a romantic
Irish postman father, an even more romantic Dublin uncle whose
letters from the Phoenix Assurance Company on headed paper
gave the impression that he moved in the corridors of power,
whereas in fact as a janitor he only moved in the corridors. There
was also an arthritic English uncle who raged about the iniquities
of milk. There was a young sister to be taught by the author
himself, inclined to pedagogy as he was, with the aid of 'a small
blackboard and an overbearing manner'. Above all there was the
patient one, mother, who was half a realist and half a Niobe.
Here is the one side, practical, disillusioned, steady:

My father claimed to be descended from a king
Called Brian Boru, an ancient hero of Ireland.

My mother said that all Irishmen claimed descent
From kings but the truth was they were Catholics.

We would have preferred to believe our father.
Experience had taught us to trust in our mother.
('Anglo-Irish')[17]

and here is the other, classical, tragic:

She was bending over the kitchen sink,
Milk, warm and unwanted, draining away,
Milk mingling with tears – or so I now think.
('A Glimpse')[18]

[15] *Ibid.*   [16] *Ibid.*   [17] *Ibid.*   [18] *Ibid.*

In the group, not in the egotistic centre, perhaps slightly to one side in an indirect light, stands the author himself, clearly loved and looked after. He was in childhood subject to recurrent and unyielding dreams, he was incessantly medicated with the splendid-sounding remedies of the period, brimstone and treacle, powders in strawberry jam, California Syrup of Figs, Parrish's Food, Senna tea, Cascara sagrada, Ipecacuanha Wine. Not only his germs but his teeth were under constant assault, from treats like chewy locust, thick strong liquorice sticks, aniseed balls, bull's-eyes and sherbet. He and his sister believed in a natural order according to which mother should be in the house and father out of it. If they were not, they would flirt in a queasy fashion, or quarrel or be sick. The author was a bookish boy who learnt to read the old newspapers lining the copper upside down, who achieved a puzzled family fame at an early age by rescuing a broken-backed Bible from the dustbin, and who read *The Well of Loneliness* at the age of 10 and never forgot it, though it seemed to be a very different book when he read it at the age of 40. Sex for the child meant another enemy, quarrels or mysterious troubles or a man frightening his little sister or another getting angry at him in a public lavatory; as he grew up it continued in its vagueness. He does not remember learning about sex in the school lavatories though he did remember the lavatories.

> It was homework and rugger; then
> It was essays and walks to Grantchester.
> Perhaps we were great Platonic lovers then.
> Perhaps there is nothing to remember.
>
> ('Ugly Neck')[19]

Religion was hardly more engaging:

> In Sunday school a sickly adult
> Taught the teachings of a sickly lamb
> To a gathering of sickly children.
>
> ('Sunday')[20]

In church it was 'grim buffoonery' relayed by bad actors radiating insincerity:

> Strange, that a sense of religion should
> Somehow survive all this grim buffoonery!
> Perhaps that brisk old person does exist,
> And we are living through his Sunday.
>
> ('Sunday')[21]

[19] *Ibid.*   [20] *Ibid.*   [21] *Ibid.*

It was also, as taught, ugly and distinctively non-feminine:

> It was the undefended one felt for.
> On the third day
> He arose from the dead and no doubt was
> Well received at Heaven's gate.
> He was on secondment. At no time
> Was he ignorant of his state.
>
> His ignorant bewildered mother
> Was another matter.
> In our street the pangs of labour
> Were nearer than those of crucifixion.
> Carpenters were useful, but
> Every family required a mother.
> The dirty end of the stick was known to us;
> Nine months for a start
> In an unskilful posture.
>
> Because of the fear of Rome, we
> Hadn't heard too much about her.
> Our Church was run by married men;
> They were minded to put her away privily...
>
> ('Religious Phase')[22]

The touch of regret and dry affection for religion, scornfully rejected elsewhere, witnesses to the ripeness of Enright's personality and the inclusiveness of his attitude. He is, and not always at different times, radical, conservative, liberal, superstitious agnostic, sceptical theist, intellectual, comedian, wit, critic, poet, humanist. In one poem in *The Terrible Shears*, 'Times Change', Enright reports that while he had many complaints in youth one thing he never complained of was being misunderstood.

> That in fact was what, if ruefully, one hoped for.
> To be understood would have been calamitous.

But in these mild, quiet poems he has perfected a style so lucent, clean and bare of ornament that it would be impossible to misunderstand him, just as he has arrived in the poems of the last seven years at a humanism so mature, sensitive, independent and unprejudiced that it would be, in these hard, inhuman times, a calamity not to understand him.

[22] *Ibid.*

BIBLIOGRAPHY

A Commentary on Goethe's 'Faust'. New York, New Directions, 1949.

The Laughing Hyena and Other Poems. London, Routledge, 1953.

Academic Year. London, Secker and Warburg, 1955. To be reprinted by Woburn Press in 1974.

The World of Dew: Aspects of Living Japan. London, Secker and Warburg, 1955; Chester Springs, Pennsylvania, Dufour, 1959.

Editor, *Poetry of the 1950's: An Anthology of New English Verse*. Tokyo, Kenkyusha, 1955.

Literature for Man's Sake: Critical Essays. Tokyo, Kenkyusha, 1955.

Bread rather than Blossoms. London, Secker and Warburg, 1956.

Heaven Knows Where. London, Secker and Warburg, 1957.

The Apothecary's Shop. London, Secker and Warburg, 1957; Chester Springs, Pennsylvania, Dufour, 1959.

Editor, with Takamichi Ninomiya, *The Poetry of Living Japan*. London, Murray, and New York, Grove Press, 1957.

Insufficient Poppy. London, Chatto and Windus, 1960.

Some Men are Brothers. London, Chatto and Windus, 1960.

Addictions. London, Chatto and Windus, 1962.

Editor, with E. de Chickera, *English Critical Texts: 16th Century to 20th Century*. London and New York, Oxford University Press, 1962.

Figures of Speech. London, Heinemann, 1965.

The Old Adam. London, Chatto and Windus, 1965.

Conspirators and Poets. London, Chatto and Windus, and Chester Springs, Pennsylvania, Dufour, 1966.

Autobiographical sketch: in *Midcentury Authors*, New York, H. W. Wilson Company, forthcoming.

Unlawful Assembly. London, Chatto and Windus, and Middletown, Connecticut, Wesleyan University Press, 1968.

Selected Poems. London, Chatto and Windus, 1969.

Memoirs of a Mendicant Professor. London, Chatto and Windus, 1969.

Shakespeare and the Students. London, Chatto and Windus, 1970; New York, Schocken Books, 1971.

The Typewriter Revolution and Other Poems. New York, Library Press. 1971.

Daughters of Earth. London, Chatto and Windus, 1972.

Man is an Onion. London, Chatto and Windus, 1972; New York, Library Press, 1973.

Foreign Devils. London, Covent Garden Press, 1972.

The Terrible Shears. London, Chatto and Windus, 1973.

Rhyme Times Rhyme. London, Chatto and Windus (in press).